NATURE'S LARDER

NATURE'S LARDER

Cooking with the Senses

Written and photographed by

DANIEL DE LA FALAISE

RIZZOLI
NEW YORK

New York · Paris · London · Milan

For Molly

Curiosity is the cure for boredom.
There is no cure for curiosity.

PART ONE: ESSAYS

PART TWO: RECIPES

FINGER FOOD & COCKTAILS
page 63

SOUPS & BROTHS
page 87

SAVORY FIRST COURSES
page 115

RISOTTI E SPAGHETTI
page 142

SCALES & SHELLS
page 171

FUR, FLEECE, FEATHERS & HIDE
page 197

ICES
page 227

AND A FEW MORE
page 249

On the moor with Papa and Dell, 1977

I.

FIRST BITE

My sister and I were brought up at the Bailey surrounded by animals in harmony with the seasons and conditioned to the value of water, silence, space, and fresh air. Our senses were cultured to ingredients grown in live soil, to kitchen life and the conviviality of the table. Mother kept a garden and fed us a bounty of herbs and greens, roots and flowers. Occasional meat or poultry, vegetables, bread, milk, and honey—all home grown—were as abundant or as scarce as Mother Nature, ingenuity, and luck permitted.

The Bailey is a farm flanked by three hills perched atop a dingle in Radnorshire. A lane of elder, rowan, and hazelnut lead to the hill gate and the moor beyond. A few hundred yards further on, discreetly emerging from a bank of heather and bilberries, runs a spring of crystal clear water which within yards becomes a generous flowing pebbled brook carrying *blue gold*—water filtered through moorland peat and slate—to the valley below and the river Wye.

Years of my childhood were spent ankle-deep building dams and playing along Col-Brook's meandering course; down through the fields, along the lane, under the beech and sycamore shading the yard, and on across the ford, downstream. You could put your face to it and drink it up. The house was plumbed from the spring on the hill; we bathed in it and cooked with it.

Radnorshire in the 1970s—Welsh border country—was a place largely ignored by progress. Bareback shepherds and vintage tractors provided the local brawn; lambing, sheep shearing, and haymaking were the year's marquee events. The valley harbored a close-knit community, albeit one shaped by the wisdom, feuds, and folklore that characterize rural life.

I was only nine years old when I would take off on a motorcycle across the moors. Free, I could ride for miles in any direction along drovers' paths, through hill air, towards rain in valleys ahead that would dance upon the wind only to be swept aside for sun. It was a landscape of heather, bracken, and gorse, interspersed with springs and streams. There were few signs of mankind.

Bantams, ducks, and geese had free rein over the orchard, lane, and stream until dusk—or until their necks were wrung. We had hundreds of sheep who bore hundreds more lambs. March and April mornings began with a border collie to heel and a tail count of the new born.

The lamb we ate was often an orphan, reared in the kitchen whilst frail, then castrated and kept in the farmyard among feathered and cleft-footed friends to fatten for the table. The months of trust and regular meal times that were the relationship's cornerstone would come to an unsuspected and abrupt halt; always at night, with a bullet to the back of the head and a knife to the throat. My father, Alexis, would bleed the lamb over the stream. Then he would hang, gut, and skin it in the barn. These were my first lessons in butchery:

dissecting animals while they were still warm, separating the joints and cuts by muscle group before rigor mortis set in.

Here, *au Tibas*, the farm I now call home in southwest France, it is something I still do. My neighbors the Vernes fatten a pig, and come January we kill it. During three days of resourceful labor and conviviality, we process larder staples for the year ahead. Every last morsel of the pig is used. Prime cuts of *jambon de pays*, shoulder, and bacon are doused in moonshine and cured with salt. The carcass is scraped and sausages are minced and seasoned; salami, brawn, and paté are made. Everything from the trotters to the snout is rendered down slowly in a huge copper cauldron over the fire. The remaining fat is strained and reserved in sterilized jars; it is this fat that the Vernes and many of their peers use for cooking year-round.

Roger and Huguette Verne met at school and were married just after World War II. They were so relieved when the Nazis left that they opened a ballroom in their barn and for the ensuing decade people from miles away would flock there on bicycle and foot for dancing, drinking, cards, and chaperoned flirting.

A simmering cauldron of soup graces the Vernes' hearth from autumn to spring. Together with their neighbor and childhood friend, Monsieur Blanc, they are a fountain of peasant wisdom. I call them the "Pre–Marshall Plan Gang." They live the way they grew up: timelessly and autonomously.

The term "peasant" here has no derogatory connotation. There are those who proudly claim the identity of peasant, and project it as a mark of their values and rural cultural identity. *Paysan* in French means "one from the countryside." It takes its root from *pays*, and descends from the Latin *pagus*, referring to an area controlled by a tribe.

In peasant farming communities, the identity of a producer is often colored by the nature of a crop and the vernacular of a geographic region. Southwest France is known as *le Verger de La France*, the Orchard of France, because of its fruit. The passing down of inherited skills, actions, and of ways of doing through bloodlines and groups of workers has a wonderful way of enabling distinct identities to form. Generations of peasant agriculture give us the Peach Man, the Cider Family, the Oyster Girl, Mrs. Melon, Mr. Moonshine, *Mademoiselle Miel*, and so on. They form a kaleidoscope of characters that all emanate the spirit and nature of their product, and by association, the culture of their region.

In an agricultural context, at least in France today, there is a clear line between those that employ age-old natural methods—often at a family scale—and those who embrace the progressive techniques of industrial farming. Peasant-scale agriculture that employs natural methods in unspoilt environments enables a sensorial reference for ingredients of vitality to persist. It represents a flavor bank of sorts.

In wine-speak, *terroir* is a term employed to describe the particularities of a wine: grape variety, quality of soil, microclimate. It refers to the component parts and contributing factors that make up the whole. The roots of the vine penetrate the earth and reach for the soluble minerals of the rock below; the result is that you taste the *terroir*. The same applies to cheese, cider, fruit, vegetables, and so on: the quality of the diet that a dairy herd

Monsieur and Madame Verne, 2014

feed upon directly affects the quality of the milk they produce. Natural, home-grown, chemical-free, flower-rich spring hay will manifest itself in the cheese. It will bring richness to the milk and the various grasses will qualify flavor and color. In the same way, the milk of an industrial hormone and antibiotic-pumped herd fed on a processed diet will transfer its distinguishing qualities to a cheese.

There are a multitude of regions where peasant-scale farms persist and produce is still grown by natural methods. Whose terroir offers conditions favorable to the production of a particular type of farming. To partake in the sensorial reference of a Cavaillon melon, a Normandy apple, a Brittany lobster, salt marsh lamb, a Gaillac peach, Nantes carrots, a prune from Agen, a sausage from Toulouse, and so forth and so on, is to participate in our sensorial heritage. It is identity affirming, joyous, and sensual.

The foundation of my work as a cook is the vitality and integrity of the produce I use. I am particular about the health of the soil in which vegetables are grown, the quality of the pasture that livestock graze, and the integrity of waters from which fish are caught. I want to know where an ingredient was grown, by whom, and how.

So when sourcing food I do just that: I go to the source. I buy direct from a producer and wherever possible skip the middleman. I have made many friends through first having discovered their produce. If the ingredient projects vitality and appeals to the senses, it is likely the result of a wholesome process. Establishing relationships with the people and environments that grow and rear what you eat has a subtle but significant effect: it encourages the endowment of respect to the food that graces your table.

To bring the perfect peach or the freshest cheese from the milk of one herd to a far-flung, unsuspecting table and the palates of so-called "sophisticates" brings me—and all those involved in the reassuringly short food chain—great pleasure. Such simplicity is in my experience what constitutes true luxury.

I first learned to cook by spending time with my family in the kitchen. My family is neither French nor English—we are both. Our approach to cooking is a celebration of raw ingredients and involves as little interference as possible from the cook. The art of seasoning and an awareness of the synergies that occur between different ingredients were instilled in me at an early age, as was the notion that every vegetable keeps a mistress in the herb garden.

Something cooked "*à la* Great-Grandma Rhoda" conjures up fantasy and daring. Rhoda was just as committed to her garden and easel as she was to her kitchen. She was notorious for making lobster bisque to feed her rose bushes, sparing neither herbs nor brandy. Yet her great contribution was to create a picture-book vegetable garden in a valley between the Long Man of Wilmington and the Litlington White Horse at Charleston, a stone's throw from the sea in Sussex. This garden is the *mother garden* of the paternal side of the family. It is where Rhoda passed on her green fingers and discerning palate to future generations.

Grandma Maxime was a passionate cook. She was taught and inspired by her mother, Rhoda, to try anything in the kitchen at any hour of the day, often under the eye of her father, Oswald. Oswald was himself an exacting cook. He ate his way across the length and breadth of France at the turn of the century while an art student. He then had a career as a

Lady Rhoda Birley, Charleston Manor, c. 1970

portrait painter to the Royal Court and the general high and mighty, which swept him—often with Rhoda at his side—through the grandest dining rooms of the British Empire. The garden and woods at Charleston happily yielded plentiful rations. There were rabbits, pigeons, chickens, vegetables and fruit from the garden, and local fish from the sea.

After World War II, Maxime moved to Paris, where she married my French grandfather, Alain. She described post-war Paris as one unending adventure in taste. A time of euphoria, of freedom wrestled back from Nazi grip. They dined in private houses, artists' studios, great restaurants, and tiny roadside bistros across France.

Alain was an authority on the bachelor menu. For years he orchestrated the seasonal menus for his canteen, the Jockey Club in Paris. During their short marriage Maxime and Alain shared two great passions: one was a party, the other food.

Maxime had an eye as sharp as a jay and a capacity to absorb influences and re-interpret them as her own in a single breath. As effortlessly as she would sketch the bones for a ball gown, she'd invent a dish—that she'd at best daydreamt—and, hit or miss, serve it as a staple classic. In the seventies, Maxime wrote a book on medieval cookery, *Seven Hundred Years of English Cooking*, and was known for shamelessly subjecting everyone in her path to the trials, errors, and occasional triumphs of her kitchen. *À la Maxime* is a euphemism for attention to the detail of the exotic.

Alexis, my father, would turn his hand from carpentry to farming, to gardening, to cooking, to his studio and drawing board. A master of the art of seasoning, he always kept an impeccably clean and orderly workstation. In spite of years in fancy restaurant kitchens, I have yet to meet a better saucier, or roaster of meat and fish. I did my first apprenticeship at his side, peeling and chopping as his *commis*. He gave me my first chef's knife for my seventh birthday in exchange for a penny.

It came from E. Dehillerin in Paris, a paradise of copper cookware and *batterie de cuisine* that has been in business since 1820. It stands on rue Coquillière, a street that once bordered Les Halles, the old food market in the center of Paris. Great-grandpa Oswald went there, as did Maxime and Aunt Loulou, and as do I at the slightest excuse.

We enjoyed the occasional influx of magnums, Camels *sans filtre*, and caviar that were brought to us by glamorous relations and family friends from London, Paris, and New York, but the backbone of our larder at the Bailey was dutifully provided for by graft and wits.

My sister, Lucie, and I were put to work in the garden at a young age. Our parents would help us plant rows of vegetables that we grazed on like rabbits until we were given plots of our own. I was passionate about artichokes, every variety I could find. I planted seven by seven rows of violets to eat raw, whoppers to steam, and an ornamental flowering line, all fenced in by elephant-eared rhubarb.

Proper grazing is done on site, between rows of produce in a garden, in an orchard, or along a hedgerow. It is the act of tasting as you forage. It is quite the antithesis of picking, which implies selecting from a previously gathered assortment. My keen grazing soon revealed to me artichoke's affinity for nearby growing parsley. I realized that when eaten together, their flavors fuse to become a delicacy.

As my garden and palate evolved I always strove—and still do—for simple, clean, sensual cooking that celebrates natural synergies. This is how I began my journey of sensorial discovery: asparagus and tarragon, artichoke and parsley, tomato with young lovage. Growing up, the kitchen was always the place to be. The heart of the house, it was where the action was, a place of congregation, nourishment, and communion. Generosity and equality have a way of emerging in kitchens as people gather around fire, clink glasses, and break bread over soup.

Wherever you are and whatever time of year it is, there is always an edible ingredient at the peak of its season. It may just be an herb or a flower to accompany something salted, smoked, and prepared during a previous glut, but nevertheless, it will indelibly mark the moment in time and place of your meal. It is the quality of this memory, its sensorial quality that will accompany you through time.

I was brought up paying attention to the texture, flavor, and taste of foods harvested and eaten instantly. A first bite of asparagus cut from its bed, a freshly caught fish filleted and eaten raw, or a white peach bitten while still warm from the afternoon sun. The flavor, texture, and taste of ingredients savored at the very peak of ripeness and desirability creates a sensorial point of reference. Rich subtleties inform the senses and remain; they act as guide, stimulus, and sensory triggers to the imagination—to what I call the *mind's eye and palate*.

When you combine a reference to the essence, flavors, textures and tastes of ingredients with the awareness of how to best celebrate the natural synergies that occur between them, cooking crystallizes into a sensorial vision. Where there are no rights or wrongs, merely what you aspire to taste.

Cherries may be late and there may be few, but you can be sure they will come, and perhaps by happy accident—and for the briefest of moments—coincide with the tender leaves of early basil. The question you must ask yourself is, "What have I got and what can I do with it?" Well if the mind's eye and palate are curious and alert, the answer is: whatever you aspire to taste. A few blanched and shelled broad beans, a handful of stoned cherries, the leaves of young, tender basil, a pinch of salt, and a splash of good olive oil: a few odds and ends become a delicate spring garnish.

If you can imagine that when you eat food that is the product of a system, you ingest both physiologically and emotionally the values of that same system, it makes sense that to pick and eat a perfectly ripe apricot is to be at one with the fruit, the tree, the orchard, the season and nature. In the same vein, when you eat a processed food, it follows that the values you ingest are those of uniformity and eternal global summer. A world where the season, the farmer, and everyone involved in the industrial chain producing that food disappears into an underpaid and faceless background haze. Processed food is disconnected from the place, the person and the methods that enable its production.

The way that food has come to be grown and then moved around the world is fuelled with energy extracted from finite fossil fuels. This dependence has enabled us, as a species, to become disconnected from the rhythms of our planet and diminished our sensitivity to the balance of an environment that manifests itself in cycles of birth, growth, death, and rebirth—as Mother Nature proceeds through the seasons of the year. A wheel of life has been compartmentalized into segregated lines of intensive industrial production. Age-old methods of agriculture based on balanced biodiversity have been replaced by monoculture. Crops are designed for productivity, uniformity, and durability; neither flavor nor texture gets much of a look in. The priorities are fruit and vegetables that will withstand mechanical harvesting, transport, and storage. Thus a few varieties are prioritized, and diversity—nurtured and passed down through generations—is cast aside.

Land is impoverished through intensive agriculture. A system of artificial fertilizers and chemicals is unsustainable. Yields soon peak only to fall, as the soil, increasingly diminished, requires ever more chemical support to function. Land that has more taken out of it than is put back in ultimately reaches a point at which it no longer supports life. Regions in the world where great civilizations flourished have often benefited from a process of natural soil replenishment, enabled by fortuitous geography and the nutrient and mineral-rich overflows of rivers. Rivers are the veins of an ecosystem. Great rivers carry fertilizing humus and rich soil from high interior mountain sources down to the sea. This fertilizes the soil, makes agriculture possible, and enables the river's borders to sustain population. To compromise a river's source, or dam its path, is to choke a nutrient-carrying artery. Deforestation destroys the root systems that filter, enrich, and gently release rainwater downstream. It leads to flooding and ultimately, desertification.

When tilling a plot of land, a garden, even tubs upon your windowsill, you soon formulate a list of priorities: fertility of the soil, exposure to sunlight, and proximity to clean water for irrigation. Then you need seed stock to plant. The advent of Genetic Use Restriction Technology rings a death knell to diversity. This patented commercial seed that commits suicide after one harvest means that the control held by plant breeders has become total. Growers are required to purchase seed for each season's planting. This is an unprecedented challenge. The very definition of food sovereignty is the ability to save seeds from one season to the next. Just ask Monsieur Verne about tomatoes. He is eighty-five and since he was a kid he has been judiciously selecting and improving seed stock from one season to the next. He who controls the seed controls the food. Land, water, and seed stock: the historical realm of the peasant, these are emerging as the battle lines of globalization. All whilst peasant culture, its vital skills and know-how, evaporate into the ether.

At the Bailey I was lucky. I knew what the sheep that I ate—ate, and whence the water I drank came. Nowadays I know what the Vernes' pig eats, and what and where their bantams peck and lay. The manure that these animals deposit is a valuable resource. It replenishes the soil by replacing borrowed minerals and nutrients. The simplest, oldest and surest method of maintaining healthy live soil is achieved through the responsible management of prairie using plants and animals. That is to say, farming (or gardening) a controlled environment with design and staying ever attuned to nature's rhythms and cycles.

Crops are best sown and harvested in cyclical rotation on parcels of land that are intermittently grazed, trodden, and manured by livestock. Carbon, oxygen, hydrogen, and nitrogen that are taken from the soil by plants return to the soil as manure and biodegradable plant mass. This cycle regenerates and replenishes the soil for a new generation of plant life to draw upon. Managed efficiently, at its own rhythm, this simple, balanced and natural system optimizes the transference of solar energy and enables the creation of soil. Like preceding generations of plants and animals, we rely upon soil for sustenance, and it remains necessary for the survival of future generations.

II

A BALLOON RIDE THROUGH THE SEASONS

I am just back from market. Today, April 1, on the back of a clement fortnight, spring equinox and the full moon, marks the start of asparagus season. A very precise and elegant lady appears at the same spot year in, year out and her stall is preyed upon by those in the know. She sells only what she can grow and pick herself. She has a succession of varieties throughout the short season: white, green, and wild. She picks at dusk and arrives to market by dawn, sets up her stall and scales, and sells out by ten. Expediency from garden to table is the key to savoring the full potential of seasonal produce.

Here at Tibas, tarragon is pushing up its tender young shoots and the asparagus bed has a speckling of tentative spears. A day or two longer and there will be enough for a ritual breakfast. A moment taken and savored just as with all the year's firsts: artichoke, broad bean, cherry, white peach, tomato, melon, apple, mushroom, walnut—the list is delectably endless.

For the next six weeks or so the asparagus bed will offer a regimented daily line for the table served raw as crudité, blanched with mayonnaise, in pasta, risotto, soup, or with eggs. Asparagus of different colors and sizes: from faintly sweet white and violet, to crisp green and bitter wild hedgerow purple. There is a moment at the height of the season when an abundance of varieties is available all at once, which makes for a feast unto itself, best served in the middle of the table for all to share.

A bed of asparagus tended to with care will yield for twenty years. For the first couple of years you should abstain from harvesting the spears; let them bolt and flower to invigorate the root stock with energy from the sun. At the end of each season the same rule applies. In June, let the spears grow waist height into an elegant bolting fan of greenery which creates a line of shade and shelter beside which to plant tender young vegetable seedlings. When the fan turns from green to gold and dies back in early autumn, cut it to the ground and feed the bed with compost and sand for the year ahead.

There has been no frost here for a fortnight, and sun and gentle rain have made for tree-planting weather. In great-grandma Rhoda's garden at Charleston, the jet stream has decided otherwise and the forecast is for a white Easter—there, asparagus is weeks away. The timing of the seasons is influenced by hemisphere, altitude, and microclimate. Unseasonal warmth may encourage plants to blossom early and grow tender young shoots only to be cruelly hit by frost before the bees can cross-pollinate them.

The link between kitchen and garden is central to my cooking; it is my point of reference. It is how I was taught. A kitchen garden provides an ever-present sensory resource, to harvest, to graze, and to glean. When I built a kitchen and planted a garden, I designed it so that I can practically reach into the herb garden from the stove. A couple of minutes armed with scissors and a trug and I am back to my pans. The bay tree is behind the house. Rosemary, thyme, summer savory, and sage border the paths. Parsley and chives grow in low hedges that lead to avenues of sorrel, coriander, dill, basil, chervil, tarragon, and lovage.

It is a simple and fine luxury to gather herbs, fruits, and vegetables and serve them within minutes. The vitality of any given ingredient at the height of its season is humbling. We give thanks to the miracle of the plenty offered by the transiting seasons, and hone our instinct, eyes, and nose to the delectable treasure trove of food energy—that is, nature's larder.

Ideally a meal should commence with the last breath of an ingredient soon to be over, consist in majority of ingredients at the height of their season, and conclude with early pickings of the next glut to come. In this way, the food shared at table becomes a celebration of a place and a moment in time.

When composing menus I draw upon a wealth of sensorial references that act as triggers to colors, flavors, textures and tastes that stand timelessly fixed upon the palate. Young shoots of lovage emerging from March soil. Honeycomb straight from the hive. Green hazelnuts prized from a thicket of hedgerow and cracked between teenage teeth.

Over the course of a year, I travel across France to Paris and London to cook for clients. In the southwest at Tibas there is a good fortnight's lead upon bud and blossom. So as I drive to and fro, laden with herbs and fruit harvested at dawn, I enjoy a bird's eye view of the evolving landscape.

Leaving behind the peach, prune, and apple orchards of the southwest, I cross the vineyards of Fronton and Cahors, and head north across the river valley of the Dordogne, winding through the scrub oak and truffle woods of Périgord to sheep and then cattle country high in the Limousin. And from there, over seemingly endless prairies stretching north, on past the majestic landscape of Chartres Cathedral, over the Loire and Seine, until rolling hills return and cider country leads to the coast.

Agriculture and horticulture are born of the marriage of soil and sunlight, with just a little help from the bees. In a sense, we can think of the food we eat as edible energy transferred from the sun. Whether it is directly in the form of plants enabled by photosynthesis, or indirectly, through meat that is derived from life forms sustained by plant life, everything in our diet is enabled by the sun. We can gauge the vitality of an ingredient by the degree to which it is the product of natural methods: grown in live soil, irrigated with clean water, and fed by natural light.

While astronomers determine the seasons according to the position of the Earth to the sun, meteorologists define the seasons by temperature. Gardeners and farmers keep all this in mind with an eye to the March and September equinoxes, the June and December solstices, the four intervening cross-quarter days, and the moon.

A phenomenon known as seasonal lag results in the most extreme ground temperatures being reached by ambient accumulation around the time of the so-called cross-quarter days. Reaching back to Celtic tradition, the cross-quarter days are the midpoints between equinox and solstice and mark moments of seasonal change in the agrarian calendar. My neighbors, the Vernes, garden according to the lunar calendar; weather permitting, they sow seeds, prune trees, and harvest herbs or fruit in relation to the phases of the moon. It is a natural and ingrained reflex to them, an understanding that the moon affects moisture. As it waxes, the moon's gravitational pull draws sap upwards, and as it wanes so sap descends. There are those who go even further and follow the moon's astrological position as well as its phase. These farmers assign plants to certain astrological signs and time their gardening accordingly.

At the winter solstice the sun is at its lowest zenith in the midday sky. This is cauldron, crockpot, and one-pot-wonder season, when hearty and spirit-warming food suggests itself. Persimmons ripen after the first hard frosts and bring a welcome splash of color to the winter kitchen, as do radicchio, pomegranates, tangerines, and blood oranges. Parsley, dill, spinach, leeks, cauliflower, and cabbage defiantly withstand frost. Roots and tubers carefully stored in soil or sand bring variety of flavor and texture. The winter solstice marks the shortest day of the year and symbolizes transition, from the end of one completed solar cycle to the birth of the next.

Like Christmas, the winter solstice symbolizes rebirth. The ritual of celebrating the New Year manifests itself in feast: turkey, goose, game, truffles, oysters, and lobsters; credit cards, gadgets, debt, and alcohol. Stomach-churning degrees of gluttony have become the norm. The welcoming of a new solar year through the rituals of sacrifice, slaughter, and feast has become somewhat overwhelmed and diluted of meaning by commercialism. So be it. Though gourmandize is quite distinct from gluttony and greed; rituals and feasts require fine-tuning.

This is a time of year when one is still acclimatizing to the damp and bitter cold of winter. It is the time for the larder. Jars of sauces, pickles, preserves, jams, herb-infused vinegars and oils that hark back to summer sun bring cheer to the table. At the Bailey, we often hung mistletoe above the larder door at Christmas, sowing a seed of life for the year to come. If your larder is well stocked, winter is a playful and inventive time for cooking.

The midway point between winter solstice and spring equinox falls around the second of February. The Celtic *Imbolc* and the American Groundhog Day welcome the first whiff of spring. Around this time, the first snowdrops emerge and remind us of the earth's fertility. And as the sun rises higher in the sky, shadows diminish, and the days subtly begin to lengthen.

Bitter salads—radicchio, frisée, and escarole—are at their best. Rocket and parsley begin to bolt and tender sprigs abound. The sap in fruit trees begins to rise with the moon and the prune family of damson, mirabelle, and plum lead the way. A gradual awakening occurs, and orchards and gardens progress toward bud.

This is the time to transplant trees and restructure gardens and orchards whilst they are still dormant, holding their life force in their roots. Without leaves you see the bones, the architecture of a planted space. I have come to love this time of year, of green-fingered midwifery and gradually awakening soil. Around this time the Vernes and I kill a pig they have fattened throughout the year. It is fed on a diet of produce from the garden, topped up with leftovers and spoilings boiled up into swill. Then, one nominated—often-frosty—morning, a fire is lit in the barn and we mount tripods with great cauldrons of water.

The pig is led across the yard from his sty, and a chain is gently attached to his hind ankle. In one swift action he's hoisted aloft as a knife is brought to his throat. The whole business takes very few minutes, and we embark at a pace upon three long days of work and conviviality. The offal is eaten at lunch a few hours after it was pumping and filtering blood through the deceased beast's body. Spatchcocked kidney grilled over an open fire, brushed with oil and sprinkled with salt and rosemary, provides a simple yet unbeatable sensorial point of reference for offal: bright colored, crisp textured, and clean flavored; with no hint of the lurking aftertaste that less fresh offal imparts.

We still crave soups and stews at this time of year, and with the garden awakening you can start to garnish them with the young shoots of perennial herbs. Cold winter waters means shellfish season, enjoyed live and poached, in pastas, broths, and risotti. Start by trying something raw, then sear it or steam it. There are no rules, only what you aspire to taste. Season it this way or that and gradually develop a reflex as how best to cook with whatever you have to hand.

At the spring equinox the power of the sun is increasing and we shift focus to the sowing of seed. The vegetable garden at this time of year yields delicate and bittersweet young shoots that make for unbeatable herb salads. This is a defining few weeks for gardener and farmer. Orchards blossom and clement weather will optimize pollination and enable a fruitful harvest. Young shoots, encouraged by heat, grow rapidly yet remain vulnerable to hard frosts. Each year varies, and Lady Luck determines whether we get the gentle night rain and warm afternoon sun we desire.

On the first of May, halfway between spring equinox and summer solstice, we come to *Beltane*, or May Day. Every dawn brings seemingly ever-increasing energy and light. As the sky draws each day longer the earth responds with growth, and we sense our spirits rise and life itself seems amplified and fertile. May Day marks the start of summer. This is a time to celebrate regeneration of life and the fertility of the soil; a time to wish seeds sown strength and safe journey for the season ahead. Leaves unfurl and the race is on to get all seedlings planted out.

Folklore says that the second week of May is watched over by *les Saints de Glace*, the Ice Saints, who evoke a warning of the last frosts of spring occurring under a pink moon. It is deemed prudent by the elders to plant out delicate seedlings only once this date has passed. It is a gambler's sport. I see them at market throughout the month of April: determined old geezers buying an early tomato plant or two, as their cautious wives berate them for being foolhardy. Sometimes they win, sometimes not—that's what makes it fun. Gardening is alive and variable, driven by the sun.

The vegetable garden and orchard yield broad beans and dill, peas and mint, and before long, cherries and early basil. As a row of seeds germinates and then starts to grow, endeavor to thin the young plants to regulate spacing and optimize growth. Warm salads of baby vegetables and delicate dishes of early thinnings at this time of year are at their very best.

At the summer solstice, the sun reaches its apex in the midday sky and its maximum power. Peaches come into season, as do tomatoes and melons. The time for growing is done. From here on out, produce ripens. Mother Nature goes into labor and harvest begins. It is the longest day of the year and the turning point at which light begins its gradual retreat towards winter.

In the beginning of August, halfway between midsummer and the autumn equinox, we come to *Lughnasadh* or *Lammas*: harvest time. At this point in the agrarian year, the focus shifts towards optimizing the harvest. As with blossom and pollination in spring, this is a crucial period for agriculture. Violent storms have a habit of occurring around mid-August, and if they bring hail they can devastate a pristine vineyard or field of melon in minutes. Once again, we court Lady Luck and clement weather. The right conditions will enable a fine vintage and a bumper crop. At the Bailey—it being Wales—summer arrived late, if at all. We harvested our honey from the heather on the moors. Robin, the bee-keeper, would shuttle back and forth, immune to stings and smelling of smoke, tending to the hives sheltered along the edge of the little meadow between the stream and the lane.

The days ever so slightly shorten and the sun radiates less heat from lower in the midday sky. The first signs of autumn are felt on the wind. A glut of peaches and tomatoes arrives. More zucchini, melons, and figs than one can eat. It is time to cast one's mind forward to stocking the larder for winter ahead with jams and chutneys, herb-flavored vinegars, oils, and preserves. If you are productive at this time, it will bring joy and light into the depths of winter.

The Vernes reminisce about harvest being like a dance of musical tables between all the farms. The polar opposite of today, where you have a GPS-guided soul in isolation operating a combine harvester. Before harvesting was "combined," it was done by hand, neighbor helping neighbor, laboring and feasting together, giving thanks all as one. Great one-upmanship would occur between the women. Who could put on the greatest feast, whose hospitality, generosity, and style would eclipse whose? Fires would be lit and the ashes cast and returned to the fields in order to bring luck for the coming year.

As we move into September and towards the autumnal equinox, there are apples, pears, quinces, chestnuts, walnuts, and after the first rains, mushrooms. The power of the sun is waning fast, it is time to collect the honey from the hives and settle the bees in for winter. At the Bailey, the sheep would come down from the hill and be turned onto the harvested hay fields for a couple of weeks of grazing to condition them for courtship whilst the grass still grew. As the days shortened and temperatures fell, the weaker ewes would be culled from the flock.

The landscape changes color and the first leaves begin to fall. Temperatures may vary greatly from year to year. An Indian summer might mean that tomatoes ripen into late October. Basil, delicate herbs, and vegetables can continue to yield up until the first frosts. The point at which October meets November is *Samhain*, or Halloween, and marks the imminent arrival of winter. Perennial plants die back and compost themselves to soil. Pumpkins are harvested, the last green tomatoes are turned into chutney, and one feasts on delicate herbs before Jack Frost comes and spoils sport until spring shoots anew. A last blast of heat often occurs around the first ten days of November, a counterpoint to the Saints de Glace in the calendar. My French grandfather, Alain, celebrated his birthday on Halloween. As a child I remember the paradox of celebrating his birth during a time of remembering the dead. And then by my seventh birthday he too was dead, and I under-stood the connection between the two realms.

III.

NATURAL SYNERGIES

Koi no yokan is a Japanese expression that describes the sense upon first meeting someone that the two of you may fall in love. In the context of food, a natural synergy occurs when a combination of flavors eaten together transcends individual qualities to become a delicacy. Hence the notion: that every vegetable keeps a mistress in the herb garden. Think artichokes and parsley, rhubarb and ginger, wild strawberries and flowering mint, a glass of cider with a borage leaf and a slice of white peach, a persimmon seasoned with acacia honey.

A childhood of grazing on whatever was in season revealed to me a host of natural synergies that occur between vegetables, fruits, and herbs. Mother Nature's timing is impeccable. Pumpkin and sage stand strong in the face of withering autumn. Pomegranate, chervil, and chicory bring color and faint tartness to a January kitchen. Borlotti beans bridge June to July in step with the first sweet red onions and, garnished with chive flowers, make for a delectable summer garnish. August eggplant, zucchini, and tomato accompany basil as it bolts and flowers. Mushrooms coincide with pears, and ever on.

Once you have experienced a given ingredient eaten with an herb that enhances its natural flavors, or tried one seasoned in such a way that its very essence seems uplifted, eating the same thing alone and plain at a neighbor's table tastes incomplete. The day that neighbor is invited to your table, however, and experiences a true delicacy first-hand for themselves, a sensorial stimulus causes a reference point to exist, and the result is a revelation. The senses are enhanced; texture, flavor, and taste flower, to stimulate the palate crisply, with vitality, subtlety, and cleanliness. The realization dawns that the way an ingredient was savored previously was somehow ordinary, narrow, and a poor substitute for the real thing.

Compositions of seasonal colors, flavors, textures, and tastes complement, contrast, and enhance one another. To pick a young artichoke, pare it down and eat it raw, seasoned with good olive oil, fleur de sel, and chased with a sprig of parsley, creates a sensation of delight. Pecorino is irresistible in autumn, when in your other hand you hold a freshly picked apple or pear.

True grazing is done on the move, on your hands and knees: weeding between lines of rocket and nibbling peppery bolting sprigs as you go. Walking through an August orchard and decadently biting into more apples than you could possibly finish; two crisp bites and a mouthful of juice. Picking broad beans for lunch, and for every handful that makes your trug, the discerning eye, spots a tender young specimen that you shell and neck, chased down with a twist of neighboring dill.

The delight garnered from such grazing changes one's outlook on eating. Suddenly it's not just broad beans and dill that seem most delicious, but food in general. You connect with the *common-sensual*, with the vitality of nature's larder. A strange sense of excitement and optimism takes over as you realize that such joy exists somewhere in the garden every day of the year.

A sensorial point of reference to ripe seasonal produce acts as a guide and triggers the imagination. When this combines with an awareness of the natural synergies that occur between ingredients, cooking crystallizes into a sensory vision, operating in two realms at once: the outer reality of the produce available, and the inner potential of your imagination to compose menus in harmony to your mind's eye and palate. The more connected you become to the inner realm, the more capable you become as a cook. The challenge is to maintain a minimum level of curiosity.

Savoring simple delicacies requires discipline and design. It is all too easy to lower your expectations and underestimate your potential. Delight is attainable—fleetingly—under the right conditions. An eternal-global-summer hydroponic tomato with a chlorine-rinsed basil leaf is a poor imitation of the real thing and it tastes that way, both pale and wanting.

From my earliest memory, the family kitchen always held an aura of fun, whether concocting ginger-scrambled eggs, an improvised "bare larder" picnic, or an elaborate formal dinner. Catch it, pick it, dig it, pluck, or skin it. Gather whatever vegetables, fruit, and herbs are abundant and in season for garnish; and corral them all from the garden or market through the kitchen to table.

One of the family kitchen laws I was brought up to respect is that of the cook's prerogative. It is customary that the cook savors the prime morsels in the kitchen rather than send them to table, where they may be lost in the mix. The cheeks of a roast sea bass or a lobster's coral; the oysters of a game bird; a crisp wing, tail, or ear picked from the spit and washed down with the first sip of a perfectly chilled bottle opened for your guests.

Seasoning your ingredients with a chosen spice or a condiment quite transforms them. A pinch, a splash, a dash, or a shaving of this or that can enhance the natural flavors of a given ingredient: a droplet of yuzu juice or lime and a pinch of fleur de sel on a slice of avocado, or a blush of bitter Campari to sweeten a tart citrus sorbet. A ripe white peach seasoned with extra virgin olive oil and fleur de sel seemingly tastes more like peach than it does alone. Add a splash of grappa to this and flavor, texture, and taste triangulate upon the palate to achieve a high and refined simplicity. I serve this through the peach months of June, July, and August as finger food, to open the palate.

When it comes to seasoning, just a few basics stored with care (airtight, out of sunlight, refrigerated once open, and so on) will widen your scope. With regards to salt, I use fleur de sel and gros sel: both products of the same process; they are sea salts sifted by hand from seawater evaporated by the sun. I use salt sparingly, preferring to season a finished dish with a pinch of the finest quality rather than load food with iodized and chemical-polluted industrial rock salt.

La fleur de sel, "flower of salt," is the name given to the first crystals that are lifted from salt beds. It is by definition a seasoning salt. Its delicate flavor would be lost if used for cooking. The crystals are of uneven size and retain certain humidity. This means that when you season a soup, for instance, the crystals do not melt, but remain intact, landing where scattered, and thus adding a textured seasoning to a dish. *Gros sel*, "big salt," is composed

of the crystals that remain once the seawater has evaporated. This I use for cooking: salting water for pasta, blanching vegetables, or cooking shellfish. Be careful not to season a soup or anything delicate with gros sel, for it is very strong. One can always add a pinch of salt, but once in, it's in.

An un-waxed lemon or lime is an asset. Herb-flavored vinegars, when concocted with care, likewise bring an element of qualified acidity to a seasoning. I use a rasp-edged grater to process fresh and dry spices: Javanese pepper, fresh ginger, star aniseed, cardamom, chili, and or any quality dry spice you desire. Saffron brings a magic blush of sun and vitality to anything from rice to broth.

Extra virgin cold-pressed olive oil is something I would miss enormously if stranded on a desert island. Fiery and peppery in late autumn when freshly pressed, it has such charisma that it almost transcends the dressed ingredient itself. A grilled sausage or a bean stew becomes little more than an excuse to serve yet more oil. As its flavor mellows over time, the oil becomes increasingly suitable for pairing with herbs: basil, garlic, bay, chili, and so on. They become allies in the larder, bringing summer sun to a winter table. Oil should be kept in a dark glass bottle out of sunlight and away from the stove. Exposure to oxygen oxidizes oil; so buy bottles of a size tailored to your use.

Olive oil is just as welcome upon a dinner or luncheon table to season fish or garnish a bowl of soup as it is at breakfast or high tea. The sweetness of honey, for instance, is accentuated by the peppery mild acidity of olive oil, and by eating the two together; you enjoy their individual flavors enhanced.

Using the honeys of different flowers allows you to garnish a dish according to season. Apple compote seasoned with delicately fragrant acacia honey at an August table harks back to spring. To season the same compote with blackberry honey, dark and deep in flavor, is to cast the spell of approaching autumn. Fall chestnuts gently poached in a spiced broth garnishing a Thanksgiving bird are something else when glazed with honey from the flower of the mother tree.

At certain times of the year, your variety of choice is limited. One makes do with hardy frost-proof greenery whilst increasingly reaching for condiments and spices that perform the task of awakening the palate. The processes of preserving and infusing allow you to bring distant seasons to the table and marry them with an ingredient presently available. *Pasta al pomodoro* in January comes from the larder: use a jar of August tomatoes seasoned with basil-flower-infused olive oil and garnish with winter parsley and rocket.

As various produce comes into season, you can often find nearby accompanying herbs that complement their flavor, and perhaps even aid digestion. Trout poached in wild fennel water and served with a watercress salad is a menu that could be foraged virtually standing still, with one arm picking wild fennel on the riverbank, another in a nearby bed of watercress, and a third tickling the trout. Chances are—if you have sharp eyes—you will spot wild horseradish growing not far away. It might sound picturesque and otherworldly, but until only very recently in human history, such activity would have been regarded as merely resourceful. The very same herb will provide an array of seasonings as it matures. Scattered around the garden I always try and maintain herbs of the same variety that are at different stages of maturation. Thus I always have to hand: the delicate young leaf, the crisp texture and pronounced flavor of the bolting sprig, the fragrant flower, and the clean fresh spice of green seed. Parsley, dill, coriander, chives, lovage, basil, and others can all be organized in this way, whether in a high-rise window box or in a bed of manured soil. You can keep them in check to a degree by ruthlessly cutting them back for your salad bowl and planting new generations at staggered intervals.

Certain vegetables, when allowed to flower and bolt, will also provide new flavors. For instance, leeks and onions have flavorful flowers that sit high upon long stalks in bulb-like pods. They open to reveal a fist of tiny flowers all packing allium family punch. Baby leeks, steamed and served with leek-flower vinaigrette, are a simple delicacy, forming a sensory rainbow arcing from delicate flavor to subtle clean taste.

Fruit is another effective seasoning with which to compose menus. In its raw state it is versatile finger food, like the aforementioned grappa-doused peach. Try an apple peeled and bathed in fresh ginger juice. A peppered strawberry with a floret of mint, a mouthful of melon and cardamom, ripe apricots and fresh almonds dressed with the flesh of a mild chili and seasoned with oil and salt. Orchard fruit roasted whole in their skins, then undressed and seasoned, become a savory vegetable accompaniment. Simply roast a pear until it just surrenders to touch. Divide it into quarters and add it to the pan juices of your roast with bay leaves and whatever herbs suit you best.

Cooking *en papillote* is a form of steam-baking wherein an ingredient is enveloped in parchment paper with herbs and spices, allowing you to retain the cooking juices. It is very effective with fruit: for instance, peel and quarter a pear, removing all inedible parts, and detail the fruit to the size and shape you desire. Add bay, ginger, chili, and whatever you aspire to taste; add a splash of oil and a pinch of salt. Fold this all up *en papillote* and it will steam-bake in the oven, creating its own juice. Keep in mind that there is a way to pare fruit and vegetables: a carrot grows lengthwise and looks distinctly carrot-like when cut accordingly; a pear grows around a core and is best divided into segments of halves, quarters, eighths, and so on.

When grilling oily fish such as fresh anchovies, tuna, or sardines over charcoal, a generous slice of grilled lime is a balancing accompaniment, as is a high summer salad of raw sweet onion, peach, tomato, and basil. This works just as well with grilled breast of veal or indeed pork.

Fruit stewed into compote makes for a digestive dessert. Try rhubarb with ginger or apple spiced with bay leaves and chili. Serve in a dainty portion at the end of a meal to clean the palate and stimulate digestion, dressed with raw yogurt, berries, and honey. Think of it like a deconstructed ice cream or sorbet, without the sugar.

There is something to be said for curious and applied grazing, and the opening of the imagination to the seasoning and combining of ingredients. It needn't be cerebral or over-earnest. On the contrary, the act of cooking should remain intuitive and playful: dandelions with rabbit and ever on.

IV.

WAYS OF DOING

I grew up reading cookery books more as tomes for virtual grazing than as instruction manuals for the following of recipes. If you long for Japanese cuisine and you are miles from anywhere, it is not a recipe that is going to sort you out. Rather, it is the basic skills and the method necessary to improvise a dashi broth. That and the foresight to stock a larder with staples and condiments that cater to your palate. Bring konbu to a simmer; infuse with bonito flakes and strain. Season with miso paste, simmer to taste and garnish with whatever you so wish. Thus in the dead of night, in a matter of minutes, with method, you have conjured a soup. If your larder is completely bare, at least you can read about it, look at the pictures, and taste it all in your mind's eye. Jot down a shopping list for the morning, roll over, and go back to sleep.

I always feel empathy for people driven to purchase a list of ingredients only to come up an ounce short and compromise quality and season. The bewilderment that engulfs obeisant-recipe followers when they can't find a listed ingredient is totally uncalled for. You are often surrounded by vastly more appetizing and fresh seasonal fare. Why not approach the situation the other way round? Cooking should be fun. When you arrive at the market, first do a lap of all the stalls. And with a mind to your budget and to those you are cooking for, build your menu around the produce that jumps at the eye and awakens your palate. Understanding provenance, seasonality, and the natural synergies that occur between ingredients will give you an intuitive sense of how to shop—which is already half the battle.

Cooking need not be laborious or difficult; what matters is proceeding with method and vision. The satisfaction gained from doing a job properly soon outweighs the energy spent. With curiosity and consideration to the integrity of the food you put on the table; think about what it is you ingest and feed to your loved ones. Success lies in being curious and caring enough to assume responsibility. If your approach is result driven it is far too easy to blame a sponge cake not rising on some recipe book. Or to be tempted to cheat and buy a chemical-ridden mix. Rather embrace the process, acquire a feeling for the texture and consistency of creamed butter, sugar, egg yolks and flour. Whip egg whites to perfect peaks, and as you gently fold them in, know the weight of citrus zest or moonshine you can add and have the cake still rise.

At Harry's Bar, Chef drummed into us at a high volume: "*Madonna Lepre* . . . you do big things with big things and small things with small things, *avete capito?*" Seemingly incomprehensible gibberish, and yet there was a thread of sense to it: a better egg will make a better cake. Chef did not mean a big recipe collection either. Recipes are a hindrance. They clutter and intellectualize what is essentially a sensorial journey. It is more practical by far to start by grasping the basics of what I call "ways of doing," or method. When you apply method to ingredient, you are free. You discover the ingredient before you and according to its vitality; you intuitively decide how to proceed.

A live scallop still quivering on the plate needs nothing more than oil and salt. A scallop that is left over and has spent the night in the refrigerator, neatly wrapped in muslin, will not have the same appeal if eaten raw. It will have lost crispness of texture and so you must adapt your method to the ingredient, and pan fry it with star aniseed, or roast it with bacon, use it for pasta, risotto, or tempura.

With an inkling of application you can soon sense when a fish is done and when a citrus sorbet is seasoned from tart to just so. *Al dente* is the precise moment that a vegetable is cooked. Not a second more and not a second less. Getting it right comes from tasting as you go, from experience and trial and error. Above all, it comes from caring and assuming the responsibility to optimize the sensorial and nutritional potential of the food you put on the table. As children, my sister and I were enlisted to help prepare and cook supper before sitting down together at the table, without fail, at the stroke of seven. It was a daily ritual that commenced in the garden: grazing, digging vegetables, picking herbs, and finally, washing up. How should I process a given ingredient and what skills do I need? Menus suggest themselves from amongst the produce available. The kitchen is a theater for instinct.

Cooking is swayed by vogues of humor, vision, hunger, and inspiration. The ingredients, and the method chosen to cook them, are ever liable to change. The cooks every gesture has its own intrinsic sensory justification. Given the same ingredients, any two people will execute a sequence of controlled actions and deliver quite different results. There is no right or wrong, merely what one aspires to taste. A cook needs to be disciplined and to be free. Success and satisfaction very much depend upon the spirit and attitude with which you approach cooking. Embracing organization gives you the freedom to focus upon extracting the essence, flavor, and nutritional integrity from whatever ingredients you have to hand. If you can be disciplined enough to be free and cook to the potential of your skills, tools, and raw materials, there is very little that can't be done.

Produce arrives to local farmers' markets throughout the year in a succession of gluts. Often, a whole bunch of stalls will be selling the same produce. Everybody has leeks, then next thing you know it is artichokes or new potatoes; and by the end of August, tomatoes are offered for a third of the price they sell for in July, and so on. The season, the region, the variety; left to her natural rhythm this is the way nature works. The best produce is often to be found on efficiently managed stalls with swift turnover. If a farmer's point of sale is the market, he wants to sell everything and head home unburdened of stock. There is always a deal to be had. The fishmonger will have struck one at dawn. His supplier will have been in turn reacting to what the boats brought in: crab, striped bass, something, mackerel one day and wild sea trout the next. A smart monger will pass the day's *glut and deal* on to his clientele. And sharp-eyed shoppers will spot such fare and with expediency converge it to table and hungry mouths.

The ideal is to consolidate sensory marvel with nutritional sustenance, to sensorally and systematically visualize the potential of produce. On market days, aim to arrive early. Get a feel for which days of the week your grocer and monger receive deliveries and from where. It is the vitality an ingredient projects that informs the cook how to best use it. Source the finest produce at the best price and use every last part of it. The art of wasting nothing is synonymous with creativity: scraps, peelings, carcasses, heads, bones, and delicate morsels gently simmered, seasoned, and brewed to your taste rise again to rejoice and nourish as finger food, soups, salad, pasta, risotti, or broth. If you are reliant on a weekly visit to a farmers' market for your produce, start to understand how to prepare and store food to keep it fresh. Herbs and salad—when pared and washed thoroughly, left to stand briefly in gently running cold water, and then stood upon an upside down plate to drain in an adequately sized bowl—will retain their vitality for a few days.

It is preferable to keep a refrigerator sparse and neat, rather than as a repository for half-opened packets and bottles. Clean it regularly with vinegar-doused muslin. The journey from processing plant, to warehouse, to supermarket, to shopping trolley, via the trunk of your car to reach your refrigerator, may incur crossing continents and time zones. System-ize meat, dairy, and vegetables from bottom upwards to minimize cross-contamination. Endeavor to stock a larder with condiments and staples, and to acquire an armory of sorts, a toolbox, a palette of flavors and textures to inspire you, to play with, and to rely upon.

Gluts of seasonal produce when knowingly transformed into sauces, jams, pickles, and conserves bring cheer and sun to a winter table. A larder, a *garde-manger* in French, a *pantry* in American, is a repository for delectable endeavors. Often a small room or a large cupboard that is conveniently adjacent to the kitchen. It forms a line of defense between you, your family, and hunger.

It pre-dates the super-sized brand-name refrigerator. Refrigerators are invaluable for stocking meat, fish, milk, cream, and butter. And nowadays just as likely to be bursting with processed foods conditioned in packets.

Larders, in contrast—those that survive—are geared to hold staples: equipped with salt-ing slabs and marble to roll pastry. Racks for fruit, vegetables, and tubers; shelves for pulses in airtight weevil-proof jars; sauces, chutneys, cordials; flour for baking; sugar, spices, anchovies, sardines, oils, vinegars, wine, cider, moonshine, et cetera. In short, sta-ples that allow you to cook from scratch and that challenge and embolden you to whisk up larder picnics on a whim.

The advent of the cauldron meant that instead of endlessly gathering food to feed a raven-ous tribe, food could be collected moderately, and seasonal gluts managed for future use. The crafting of clay into a pot raised the curtain on kitchens and introduced a life-enhanc-ing alternative to roasting over fire. Gentle simmering in a cauldron renders previously unchewable fare tender and palatable, broadening the diet to encompass foods that oth-erwise require tremendous energy to digest. A pot acts as an external stomach of sorts, which is of inestimable nutritional benefit to the toothless, both infant and elderly. Grains and roots could be gathered, pulses dried, fish and meats salted and then all tucked safely away. And so became *larders.*

In a professional kitchen you quickly learn that your lifeline to survival depends on practi-cal and efficient organization, without which you become overwhelmed by the relentless pressure and the inevitable unexpected. Cooking is a dance to an internal, sensory logic. Unless you are super-organized, you will find no joy in it. If, before you begin, you have all your ingredients prepped, organized, and laid out in front of you, cooking becomes fun, as opposed to a comedy of errors. No burning garlic as you frantically run around searching where on earth, whatever you suddenly realize you cannot find, may be. Don't waste time looking for things you need at hand, have them at hand. Think ahead, stay objective, and sequence the tasks before you. If you are organized, you are flexible, open, and free to access the joy of improvisation, to taste and season as you go, changing direction, and adjusting to your whim.

Light fingered pilfering in restaurant kitchens manifests itself amongst *commis chefs* in the constant disappearing of potato peelers and paring knives. Such pilfering is a measure of how essential it is to have the most basic "right tool for the job." Over time, assemble a *batterie de cuisine:* an armory of tools. It may sound like a grand statement but quality kitchen utensils will last generations. As I travel and cook I have a backbone of select tools with me at all times. They are allies that enable swift, fluid action. If you have the right tool for the job, you execute the task at hand and move on to the next job.

Stainless steel is an asset; it is versatile and dependable. It bounces when you drop it. It doesn't scratch or crack or oxidize. You can buff it up with a muslin cloth doused in eau de vie or vinegar to make it twinkle as new. It is virtually indestructible and your grandchildren will get just as much use out of it as you do. I treasure and use some of Rhoda's knives, Grandpa Alain's Hollywood steamer from the 1920s, and Maxime's pots and pans. They are heirlooms of a practical kind. You need a chopping board of adequate size, one that you can clean with a knife kept sharpened for just that purpose. Even better if it fits into your sink and you can bathe it in a dilution of bleach or vinegar to clean it. Collect a set of bowls, preferably stainless steel, ranging in size from small to large that stack like Russian dolls. Small ones to hold garnish and prepped ingredients as you cook, larger ones to hydrate vegetables and rinse salad and herbs.

A set of the right-sized whisks for emulsions and a fine-meshed sieve for straining broths and juices should be in your *batterie*. Line the sieve with muslin or kitchen paper and you can strain a cloudy broth clear in an instant. A roll of muslin is the sort of staple that will last a decade. It can be washed and rise again, and, doused in vinegar; it becomes the cloth that keeps your work station clean. Next time you sit at a sushi counter, watch the chef and look for the neatly folded vinegar-doused rag of muslin at his side. An essential part of one's armory, under the heading of hand extensions, is a set of large wooden spoons in different sizes for different volume pans. Choose those that look like a paddle or an oar for risotto and stirring cauldrons. Keep a clutch of stainless steel tasting spoons in regularly changed hot water at your side as you cook.

Stock your kitchen drawer with a nut cracker, garlic squeezer, mandoline, oyster knife, and ladles, large and small. An ice bucket and a cocktail shaker for obvious reasons are crucial, as are a can opener and graters of different-gauged serrated blades for obtaining a range of textures. A measuring jug, a roasting dish, and a slotted spoon for extracting vegetables and such the moment they are cooked *al dente*.

A vegetable mill processes cooked ingredients to purée and is invaluable for vegetables, mashed potatoes, and fruit compotes. Buy one with a rasp-edged, changeable blade that can cope with peel and skin. The magic of this tool is that it allows the transformation of texture from whole vegetable to purée without altering the composite structure of the vegetable itself. Do the experiment yourself. Blanch peas or broad beans and purée them in a blender: starchy glue will emerge. Pass the same ingredients through a hand-turned vegetable mill with fresh mint, a splash of pastis, and a grating of star aniseed and you will have a delicate purée.

The tools that you have to hand will determine which cooking method to best employ. You can improvise to a degree. A colander becomes a steamer, if you find a pan for it to sit upon and a lid to cover it. But a plastic-handled frying pan cannot double as a roasting dish. Cast an eye to the cookware at hand before you start so as to know by which method to best advance. Pans with metal handles that you can transfer to the oven are life enhancing. It is a very effective cooking method. You start something on the stovetop and then transfer the pan to the oven for the time needed to cook the subject through. Sear a rack of lamb or a tail of monkfish; then move it into the oven for three minutes on each side before setting it out to rest. Try for yourself; fry an egg by this method and you won't look back.

Garner a sense of the journey your ingredients will take. Pre-visualize and anticipate the various steps. If they are to be blanched in boiling water, organize a volume of water sufficient to maintain its temperature once you add cold green beans; not one so small it becomes instantly overwhelmed with cold ingredients that cause the water temperature to drop below a simmer. Blanch ingredients in batches. Have a clear vision of the degree to which you desire an ingredient cooked. Buy a timer, and then establish that broccoli needs three minutes precisely, and that's it. It is not rocket science. Texture and flavor are captured through paying attention to detail. A two-egg omelet will turn out seared and *baveuse* in the right sized pan. If you add six eggs to the same pan it simply will not work and you'll end up with a frittata, a fine delicacy unto itself, but not an omelet. Poultry scissors that cut through gills and fins, remove wings, snip ligaments or cartilage and allow you to spatchcock a bird are essential. Good ones dismantle with a fixing bolt, which allows for sharpening.

Knives are extensions of the cook's hands. Blunt knives are clumsy and dangerous. They do not cut, causing you to apply disproportionate pressure and so easily slip, which leads to bleeding. Sharp knives are tools to be respected, looked after, and depended upon. Once a knife is properly sharpened, its cutting edge needs to be maintained. Purchase a sharpening stone and a diamond dust sharpening steel and learn how to use them.

You can get by with a select few: there are five knives every kitchen needs. A general paring knife, short with a beaked blade, acts as a claw and allows for the rapid peeling and stripping of endless odds and ends. A filleting knife with a seven-inch flexible blade allows you to apply pressure to a particular center of gravity and work in a very orderly and measured manner. Such a knife is invaluable for the undressing of fruit, removing skin, peel, or pith, and of course for filleting. A general chef's knife with a twelve-inch blade can be used for everything and will become your constant companion. A deboning knife is used like a scalpel and allows one to delve to the heart of a joint between muscle groups with precision. A prosciutto knife has a very long thin and flexible blade. Its finely balanced center of gravity allows you to cut extremely thin slivers of pretty much anything.

When confronted with a bare larder and an empty fridge, when all you have is an egg, an herb and some rice, if you can rustle up an onion, a last drop of olive oil and a knob of butter—if you allow yourself to be led by your palate and intuition—you may just conjure a little feast. Open-mindedness and a sense of adventure allow you to harness the joy of cooking. It pays to apply method to ingredient, even if the method chosen is simply to leave well alone and celebrate the ingredient raw, just as it is.

V.

ESSENCE

The longer the shelf life a product can claim, the more it will have been processed. Its vitality, color, aroma, texture, flavor, taste, and nutritional integrity all diminished by exposure to high temperatures and the addition of chemicals. It is as difficult not to be won over by perfect produce, as it is easy to be put off by bad cookery. Quite distinct from sour, salt, umami, bitter, and sweet, which are perceived on the top of the tongue by the taste buds; flavor is aromatic, volatile, and ephemeral. It is picked up by the olfactory nerves on the roof of the palate and anticipated by the nose once fixed upon by the eye. You might hold your nose as you chew upon a wild strawberry, then let go and see the difference yourself.

I was brought up to follow a very simple style of cookery. In a composed menu, I want to recognize the ingredients on the plate. I want to know, what end of which season it is and where I am. Am I in the north, the south, in the mountains, or on the coast? I want flavor to flower and stimulate, and taste to lie subtle and clean. An ingredient harvested at the peak of its ripeness will impart aromas and flavors that stimulate the senses as you bite it. And, as whatever you are chewing divulges itself to nose, teeth, and tongue, your palate will be the judge of the product's freshness and vitality.

The taste of the orchard and the taste of the cold room are worlds apart. A neighbor, a strawberry farmer, uses the flagstone-floored kitchen of his grandparent's derelict farmhouse as his storeroom during the harvest. The fragrance of strawberry that hits you as you enter overwhelms the senses. The taste buds are aroused and cry out for satisfaction. The farmer's knowing eye meets your glance and more often than not, he will proudly tender a sample.

Fresh fish smells of the sea and it is distinguishable by its texture and flavor, whereas yesterday's fish smells of fish. And, as you will have noticed, is often dressed in sauce. A broth simmered gently will taste delicate and clean. One that has been neglected and left to boil furiously becomes bitter and unpalatable. Harnessing and optimizing the vitality and essence of produce requires you to employ method and care.

As impressive as I find the stylized transformation, sleight of hand, and gastronomical trapezery of individual chefs, it is not what holds my attention. Rather, I find myself drawn to the product, the producer behind the product, and the integrity of the environment in which it has grown. Strawberries and mint is a statement as vague and potentially misleading as trench coats and trilby hats. Which variety, and by which methods? Which tailor, which milliner?

To cook is to celebrate ingredients and do justice to natural flavors, to source, pair and season ingredients in ways that underscore their inherent character, texture, and fragrance. And, importantly, to focus on how to isolate and extract the ephemeral flavor of an ingredient's very essence: by gently simmering the bones of demersal fish, or the carcasses of poultry; by roasting eggplant, pear, pumpkin, or quince whole in their skins until just done. Then standing them to rest in a colander whilst collecting the resultant unadulterated cooking juices. Such juices or broths can then be used to carry the individual essential flavors into a finished dish. Enveloped in a light sauce, an emulsion made up of cooking juices, olive oils, broths, floral waters, and choice herbs.

Capturing an ingredient's essence demands a certain respect for temperature and expediency. Both chlorophyll and protein maintain integrity up to a certain temperature, above which things rapidly change. Half of the battle is to source produce grown by natural methods, and then just as much care and application is needed when it comes to cooking it. When a product is presented to you, inquire as to whence it comes and how it was made. If the process is wholesome, the producer or monger will happily enlighten you as to the method.

When you do justice to a plate of spinach, sourced and seasoned just so, it stands alone as a feast fit for a king. Pick it, wash it, and then stand it to drain. Throw into a pan over high heat a slug of oil, a bay leaf, and a slice of ginger. Add a slice of chili, a crushed clove of garlic if you so wish, and add the spinach still a little wet with a pinch of salt and close the lid. It takes barely a minute. Check it once, spoon the leaves on top to the bottom and that's it: vibrant green spinach, which retains all its vitality and flavor. Cook it a moment too long and spinach will oxidize, and green turn to bitter grey.

When I was risotto boy at Harry's Bar, Chef would have us concoct a secret weapon of sorts at the point between May Day and summer solstice, when broad beans and peas are neither quite so sweet nor so green. Place iced water and spinach into a blender and pulverize thoroughly. Empty this mixture into a saucepan and very slowly and over a low flame, and with the help of a thermometer, bring it to 145°F (63°C) exactly. At this temperature, chlorophyll separates from the fiber of the spinach leaf, and in a swift action can be gently lifted off the surface of the water with a ladle, to be strained through muslin and reserved for future use. In early May a broad bean and pea risotto stands on its own. By late June, however, a spoon of chlorophyll for color and a splash of pastis for flavor help dress mutton as lamb.

When you add live lobster to a generous cauldron of salted, boiling water, extinguish the flame, cover the pot with a lid and gently poach your lobster in the water's accumulated temperature, counting ten minutes per pound. If it continues to boil you will soon see foam and scum rise to the water's surface. Along with these evaporates the crustacean's delicate and volatile succulence. So next time the lobster-pot testosterone barbecue napalm bunch tries to take over, stand your ground and politely suggest that they set the table instead.

Distillation is the craft of extracting essence from fruits, herbs, and plants. The subject (plant, herb, or indeed fermented fruit or grain) is brought to a boil in a still, whereupon the ephemeral and volatile aromas (plus the alcohol in the case of fermented fruit or grain) rise from the boiling mass as steam. This steam is channeled away through spiraling tubes into a cooling chamber, where the aromas, alcohol, floral waters, and essential oils are captured. Eau de vie is composed of the condensed steam of fruit alcohol, together with that of the natural aromas of a given fruit. When herbs and plants are placed in a still and boiled, the steam that is lifted and captured is composed of fragrant oils and waters. As this cools it separates into floral water and essential oil. I think of floral waters rather like magic broths: they impart the clean essence of an herb and can be used to much effect as a seasoning. So perhaps make room for floral waters next to the spice shelf in your larder.

You may be familiar with the custom of adding rose water to coffee and orange water to various custard- and cake-based desserts. A little curious investigation and trial and error will open you to a further array of potential seasonings. A splash of geranium water will refresh cook's tired face, and floral water will qualify the flavor of short broths (*courts bouillons*, as they are called in classic French cookery). For instance, add a floral seasoning of tarragon or fennel to a court bouillon when poaching fish, chicken, or indeed eggs. Rosemary works for an Irish stew, sage to concoct a sauce for rabbit, or a dilution of thyme to cook carrots.

Eaux de vie when diluted with flavored syrups become liqueurs. These are traditionally drunk before a meal as aperitifs. The classics are walnut, quince, and wild cherry. A neighbor and fifth-generation distiller, "Mr. Moonshine," maintains a conservatory of heirloom tomatoes and concocts a liqueur from a blend of seventy-two different varieties, the faintest splash of which subtly enhances a tomato salad. Eaux de vie and liqueurs mixed with sparkling water and then whisked periodically until frozen, make for lively granita to garnish fruit sorbets. You make a sorbet from the juice and or flesh of a fruit. To garnish this with the extracted and captured essence of the same fruit, or of one that shares a natural synergy, brings dimension and context to a simple dessert. A strawberry frozen yogurt dusted with a granita made from wild strawberry liqueur and then garnished with fresh strawberries and mint, delivers a delectable arc of flavors and textures from the same fruit.

It is judicious to select floral waters, essential oils, moonshines, and liqueurs made from ingredients produced by natural methods, so as to avoid ingesting extracted and concentrated pesticides and chemicals all too present on commercial crops.

Applejack—apple moonshine—from an apple expressing the character of a specific variety of tree, grown in a particular quality of soil, that is allowed to fully ripen before being picked, cleansed of stalk and pips, put to ferment, and thereafter distilled, will express its *terroir* cleanly upon the palate. It sounds so simple, and in "essence" it is: time-old processes that harness nature's rhythms and deliver produce that tastes of what it is, purely and simply.

The key to simmering broth is developed further in the chapter on soups and broths. Simmering starts the moment the first air bubbles start to rise. No faster than that. Simmering allows you to cook ingredients gently with precision and care, in a way that retains succulence and integrity of texture, and to the depth of flavor you so desire. For someone who is unwell, whose sense of taste is all askew, you should serve a bowl of the lightest of chicken water garnished with a choice morsel or two of vegetables. For a growing teenager you can use a much stronger broth to enhance flavors and substantiate a soup.

"Boil potatoes" should read, "simmer potatoes." Add bay leaves and chili and whatsoever you aspire to taste. Add a line of olive oil to the cooking water to create a light emulsion, which will carry the flavors of the added herbs and spices. Bring the potatoes up to a simmer and very gently continue to simmer until done. At a point, you can even lid the pan, turn off the heat, and let the potatoes cook to doneness in their accumulated temperature. If I am going to be in the kitchen all day cooking for hours I'll first scrub the potatoes with a vegetable brush, bring them up to a simmer in their skins and then let them cook to doneness off the heat at the back of the stove with the lid on. The potatoes thus retain integrity of starch and flavor. Their inherent qualities, specific to variety and purpose, are neither leached nor dissipated.

For fruit compote, the goal is to isolate the essential flavor of a fruit. For instance, skin, core, pip, head, and tail an apple, and then slice it thinly on a mandoline. Add it to a solid-based pan over a lively heat, with a splash of mineral water—or better still, natural apple juice of the same variety.

Add whatever aromatics you wish: ginger, chili, and bay leaves work a treat. Once it reaches a simmer, place the lid upon the pan and let the compote stew over a very gentle flame to desired taste, with a keen eye to replacing the herbs at intervals before they oxidize. Remove the lid and reduce the compote to the desired consistency and that's it. Palate-cleansing, digestion-enhancing, compote that will find its place at table: breakfast, lunch, and dinner.

I first learnt to cook amongst family and then trained professionally with the benefit of great mentors at Harry's Bar. Chef's passion for produce, his dedication to refining dishes and stripping them down to their barest bones was contagious. His strokes of genius were ever speckled with wild rages triggered by the smallest detail that could erupt like bush fire. Demotion, silence. and focused industry would be left in their wake. One quickly learnt that Chef was always right (he usually was), and especially so when he was wrong.

The pastry kitchen came under the jurisdiction of Signor Aldo, a methodically precise gentleman who did his apprenticeship in the kitchens of the Savoy hotel in the fifties. The pastry kitchen was also a place of total silence, yet unlike the submarine at battle stations edge surrounding Chef, Signor Aldo's kitchen was serene, it was as if entering a private chapel within a great church. Working under Aldo meant to silently and methodically dance in step from dawn till midnight, whereas life in the savory kitchen required the swallowing of pride and the keeping of one's wits firmly footed, front of stage.

The first sign of sloppy cooking is exposed in poor standards of kitchen hygiene. You spot it a mile off, and it is one of the first things to drill into kitchen recruits. Clean hands, clean worktop, clean fridge, and fresh produce. Sensory marvel and nutritional sustenance are all very well; yet step one is to avoid food poisoning. Strict standards of kitchen hygiene are a minimum requirement. This is not to be confused with food-hygiene laws that can have the unfortunate side effect of marginalizing "traditional" produce. To standardize and homogenize is to diminish. The great wonder and marvel of the bounty of the countryside and nature's larder is the diversity it provides.

A local sheep's cheese-maker with whom I work recently did battle and lost: her signature product was deemed not to comply with hygiene standards after a "rogue" coloration was manifest in the rind of a cheese. Despite her efforts to explain that this occurred due to the effect the flower rich spring hay that the ewes were fed had upon the milk (and commissioning multiple expensive laboratory tests that confirmed this), the "man from the ministry" pettily insisted that if so, every subsequent variation in color would need to be justified by subsequent tests. She deemed life too short and pulled the cheese from production.

Yet one only has to skip back a beat in time to be reminded of all the fraudulent practices that were rife before such laws existed. Centuries of adulterated spices: marigolds in the saffron, rat droppings in the pepper and worse. Though much of this adulteration was committed by merchants and middlemen (not producers), to add value and turn profit.

Pre-industrial society had leeway for the growing, gleaning, or poaching of local food in the countryside. During the Industrial Revolution, workers left the land and their capacity to subsist along with it. Industrial towns offered cramped housing and poor systems of food-supply for a rapidly expanding urban population, and malnutrition ensued. A tidal wave of technological progress brought about railways, pasteurization, canning, and freezing. Thereafter the food supply became global: American wheat, Australian lamb, and Danish bacon all shared the table. It was a paradigm shift in food supply and the way we eat.

The degree of malnutrition found in conscripts, supposedly healthy men in their physical prime, at the outbreak of the WWI exposed an ugly truth of urban industrial life. Four in ten men were unfit for service. Nourishment became a political issue, and research lead to progress being made pertaining to nutrition. Indeed, it is often said that rationing in WWII, which was based on a nutritionally sound and balanced diet, made for a healthier population. Then the post-war era brought with it increasingly processed foods, representing yet another paradigm shift. Brand name processed foods, presented in aspirational and emotionally seductive ways, led to the alarmingly fat and diabetic world of today.

Current hygiene laws apply to the context of modern industrial agri-business practices. As most blatantly exposed in the recent scandal of horsemeat being passed off as beef in ready meals for sale all over Europe. Romanian horses, processed in Cyprus, were being conditioned into ready meals in France, shipped to retail outlets left right and center and sold to an unsuspecting public as beef-based fast food. Hygiene law produces a paper trail of traceability, which confirms that the pink slime in your burger is indeed from the carcass of such and such a beast and has been pasteurized at a given hour on such a day; that it has been frozen and is ready for eating within a window of time defined by a "Best Before" date.

Thankfully there is always a market for great produce, and peasant scale production persists. There is however certain irony in the fact that time-old natural foods have been marginalized to the extent that they are now perceived and marketed as luxury goods. Organic, grass fed, and other labels have come to be brandished as aspirational life style accessories. The game is up on "Farm Fresh"; the discerning consumer recognizes it as meaningless. The challenge for the peasant farmer is to be allowed by law to continue to farm a product, which often has been the daily bread and identity of a family through generations.

Aspire to autonomy, herbs upon your windowsill, and vegetables in your own backyard. They say that society is but three meals away from anarchy. There exists a backbone of independent producers working hard by natural methods to sustain you; they need recognition and support. Seek out whatever you can afford.

To savor the essence of a natural ingredient hits a universal note and is delectable. When you feed even the vilest of creatures something delicious you glimpse, however briefly, the inner child residing within.

VI.

CARRYING FLAVOR

Once you have successfully extracted the essence of an ingredient, the next challenge is to carry its uncompromised flavor into the finished dish, enveloped in a sauce. When you cook from scratch with fresh ingredients your options are infinite.

An appropriation of classic French cookery has filtered down to many as a default point of reference. At the Savoy Hotel in London in the 1890s, the double act of the chef Auguste Escoffier and the hotelier César Ritz set a bold and enduring standard for restaurant service. A scandal involving the usual brown envelopes stuffed with commissions of encouragement from suppliers eventually led to a souring of relations with the management. However, far from being discouraged, the two upped and set off half a mile northwest to Piccadilly where they opened their namesake Hotel Ritz, clientele in tow.

Escoffier reformed the structure by which kitchens were staffed. He established the hierarchal brigade system whereby a kitchen is compartmentalized into sections of specialized tasks, overseen by a chef whose task is to conduct his orchestra of workers in harmony with the flow of orders brought into the kitchen by the manager. This is a simplification, yet in broad terms, it is how professional kitchens have been run since.

The organization of sauces was given a similar going over. They were divided into families, the so-called mother sauces. Bound together for the most part by flour and butter. And the effect has been enduring. Subsequent generations have reinterpreted Escoffier's art, transposing it to stock cubes and dehydrated mixes tendered for sale in spruced-up packaging. Others have refined and evolved it, great restaurateurs, and then those keen cooks in every walk of life that are conscious and particular as to what they feed their families.

Escoffier teaches us how to execute *liaisons*: the action of binding sauces together with recourse to flour and butter. With the exception of hollandaise for which egg yolks and clarified butter are used, the mother sauces of French cuisine depend on roux, which is a thickening agent conjured from equal parts fat and flour. To prepare a roux, flour is stirred into heated clarified butter to form a paste. The resulting paste is then cooked through with an eye to color, and comprises "the base roux" of three family lines: béchamel, velouté, and sauce espagnole. Each in turn yields a multitude of derivative white, blonde, and brown sauces.

Roux is diluted with a stock in accordance to its color, or family, and then cooked over gentle heat to form a thickened sauce. Béchamel sauces call for barely cooked white roux and are made with milk. Velouté sauces require a little more color, and so clarified butter and flour are cooked until blonde then diluted with white poultry stock and reduced into a thickened sauce. Sauce espagnole is made with brown veal stock, which requires a brown roux. This is achieved by cooking the fats and starch for yet longer still.

It is this brown roux that is at the heart of demi-glace, which is restaurant language for gravy or sauce. Demi-glace is a reduction of sauce espagnole and brown stock; you will have encountered it to varying degrees of success in restaurants aspiring to the principles of French cuisine. In so-called classic cooking, flour- and dairy-based sauces infiltrate and fill out a vast proportion of soups, pies, and puddings, and are readily used to garnish fish, meat, poultry, and game.

Very often even more butter is relied upon to finish a dish: to give sheen and certain unctuousness. There are those to whom the prospect of butter is deemed generous and luxurious. The portly cook who wears a self-satisfied grin, as he deludes himself that "one only lives once," whilst spooning great slabs of butter into a scalding pan of innocent vegetables. The life of a fresh vegetable as it proceeds through many a good restaurant kitchen goes roughly as follows: blanch vegetables in salted boiling water, refresh in iced water, allow to dry, then sauté in clarified butter, deglaze the pan with stock, refrigerate, and reserve for service. Whereupon, to serve: sauté with more butter.

This is a practice that Monsieur Verne dismisses with a waggling finger as: "*pas intéressant.*" The Vernes use what they have to hand. They do not follow recipes; they grow food, which is eaten with expediency from field to plate. Requiring no must-have ingredient to make it taste a certain way, give it sheen or unctuousness. The food they eat has the vitality, texture, color, and flavor of fresh food grown by natural means. When they kept geese for many years it was goose fat. Nowadays it is the pork fat rendered down from the pig they kill each January. If they kept a dairy cow then there would be butter and cream. Resourceful cooking makes for the best eating.

The reference to *sauces* that I was brought up with celebrates a lighter approach, one that focuses on creating emulsions: of pan juices, vegetable, poultry, and fish broths, mineral waters, olive oils, and herbs. An emulsion is created when fat and water particles combine to become one. A mayonnaise made of olive oil whisked into egg yolk would be the classic example of a thick emulsion. And yet much lighter more ephemeral emulsions are easily conjured with just a little curiosity and instinct, the right ingredients, and the right tools.

In the pastry kitchen good butter, milk, cream, and yogurt are allies for making ice creams, puddings, and cakes, yet there is no call for encumbering the flavors of a sauce with them. "Hormonal juice of cow!" Maxime would gasp with horror. Commercial pasteurized milk is the milk of many herds jumbled together with industry standard hormone supplements and antibiotics. Unpasteurized milk is delicious; the first sip of cream from the top of the morning's milk is a childhood reference held by the transformative effect it has upon a bowl of cereal. But as a rule I do not use dairy produce in sauces, not even butter for risotto. Dairy to me is best savored alone or combined with fruit or other such and garnished with seasonings and condiments. Think wild strawberries eaten with clotted cream; a teaspoon of sheep yogurt to balance spiced apple compote. Food on the go might be a Comice pear in one hand and a slice of pecorino in the other. A dawn breakfast could consist of good coffee to wash down a seasoning of Florentine anchovy paste spread thinly upon grilled and buttered Tuscan bread.

The way to make a sauce is to simply use what you have to hand. Gently simmered broths are a means to isolate, extract, and store the essence, flavors, and nutritional integrity of ingredients. Vegetable broth is straightforward to conjure with peelings and roots, substantiated by an onion, a carrot, perhaps a leek and the fragrant stalks of the herbs destined for your salad. Then there are others that you can organize in batches episodically, and which with a little foresight and application will help you enormously. Basic instruction for these is detailed in the introduction to soups and broths. A discreet reserve of fish and poultry broths frozen into ice cubes can transform everyday cookery. When faced with a bare larder, for instance, a reserve of lobster or crab broth prized from the depths of your freezer—made from pounded heads simmered in mineral water—will lift a pilaf rice dish into a refined delicacy. I tend to use mineral water for cooking. Not to boil pasta, or poach crustaceans but certainly for broths and sauces. Seems a shame to spend hard earned dollars on the best ingredients you can find; only to pollute them with chemically treated municipal tap water.

Whatever you are cooking, think in terms of the journey ahead. The choices of ingredients, temperature, and seasoning will determine the quality of your finished sauce. Success is measured in subtleties of flavor and taste. Let me try to illustrate this with an example: sauce for a roast chicken.

Once cooked, remove the bird from the oven and turn it breasts down, bum in the air to rest. This way the cooking juices, the essence of the bird's flavor, gravitate to the thighs and breasts. Twenty minutes or so later, lift the bird from the roasting dish, allowing all excess juices to run in to the pan and join what will become the building blocks of your sauce. We could have roasted a fish, a rabbit, or an eggplant; the ambition is essentially the same. The key is in preparing the subject for the oven with a vision of the finished dish in mind. So, be sure to add nothing that will burn and create bitterness in the heat of the oven. Exercise extreme moderation with salt, and cook ingredients with precision—to doneness, allowing them to yield juice and essence as they rest.

Once you have carved your chicken you can attack the sauce. Start by angling your roasting dish onto a slant to skim off the excess fat. As always, organize all the ingredients you need before starting. Decide which herbs you are in the mood for. Perhaps rosemary and a fine dice of parsley and chervil stalks, to add another layer of flavor. If it is summer perhaps you will use basil oil, in winter you might prefer garlic.

You'll want chicken broth to hand, that you have made previously and frozen into ice cubes. Dilute a few of these cubes with a little mineral water and bring them to a simmer. (Or just use plain mineral water if you desire a lighter result.) Place the roasting tray over a moderate flame and, with a flat-headed wooden spoon, scrape any caramelized juices away from the bottom of the pan. Gradually add a little broth and start to create an emulsion between these pan fats and the added broth.

Add the rosemary, a slug of olive oil, and begin to taste and season your sauce. At this point you could add the parsley and chervil that you finely chopped. Judge how viscous you want your sauce, and add broth accordingly. Once you are happy, pour the contents of the sauce through a fine sieve and over the carved bird. Garnish with olive oil, fleur de sel, abundant fragrant herbs, and serve.

Floral waters of various herbs that enjoy natural synergies with the main ingredients can be used to great effect. For instance, floral water of tarragon added to chicken pan juices and whisked loosely together with a little olive oil will add dimension and layers to the flavor of your sauce. Think sage for rabbit, rosemary for lamb. Pan juice stretched mayonnaises are another clean way of impacting flavor. Season them with a fine dice of a freshly chopped herb that enjoys a natural synergy with the main ingredient. The usual suspects are beef and horseradish, lamb and mint, rabbit and sage, chicken and tarragon, trout and watercress, and ever on. Stretch a mayonnaise with cooking juice or broth and garnish it with herbs and fruit that complement the main ingredient. If you have leftover chicken, put it away with care and reserve any sauce that may remain on the serving dish. This, once jellified, will be the secret weapon to the tarragon mayonnaise that will lift a humble dish of leftovers to a refined delicacy.

Form a clear vision of the flavors, textures, and tastes that you are hungry for. Strive to achieve them with the minimum transformation of ingredients. Rather than boil and reduce a sauce, gently simmer and season a carefully extracted essence. Prick eggplant with a fork and place them in a hot oven to roast whole in their skins. Cooked until they only just surrender to touch, they need no more than sitting to rest. Once they have cooled, peel, generously slice, and detail them upon a serving dish. Season this with *essence of eggplant*—the juices that have run whilst the eggplant has rested—adding basil, olive oil, and salt on your way to table.

And so forth and so on. For a lobster salad with white peach, think about stretching the accompanying mayonnaise with a little lobster broth and peach juice. Garnish the mayonnaise with a fine dice of peach, offcuts of lobster and perhaps an herb.

To varying degrees, herbs and spices play a role somewhere between food and medicine. Historically, herbs have been used to heal, to embalm, season, spice, and concoct. When flavoring a court bouillon or an herb salad, the herbs and spices at your disposal can be considered as the notes of an instrument, the blending and harmony of which enable distinctive character to emerge. Garlic and parsley in duck fat, and immediately I am pretty sure where I am. Culture and region express themselves through signature use of herbs and spices. If you first define, through trial and error, the herbs and spices that make you feel well and best appeal to your palate, the next step is to organize how to provision yourself with a constant supply. A little of the best will more than suffice. A pot upon a windowsill is a start: seed and soil, water and light. There is very little that cannot be done.

The objective is that the flavor and texture of the main ingredients upon the plate stand enhanced, by the fragrant essence of the very same ingredients, subtly omnipresent in the guise of sauce.

Maxime de La Falaise, New York, 1973

VII.

CONVERGING TO TABLE

Grandma Maxime cooked until she dropped, and her menus remained ever exotic through the years. She gave dinner parties in Paris in the forties, at Lacoste in the south of France in the fifties, and in New York from then on. First on Jane Street, then Riverside Drive, and by the time I started to help her in the kitchen it was the eighties and she lived in a long L-shaped loft on Fifth Avenue with a view to the Empire State Building.

She had three of the vilest dogs you could ever meet, whom she worshiped disproportionately. As the seventies became the eighties, Maxime's reputation for poisoning people with medieval concoctions receded, and stories of feral canines and tetanus jabs began to circulate. Feared and loathed by all, they were scrawny mongrels and discerning biters who chose their prey with cowardice and cunning. They would stay to heel on their constitutional around the little park in front of the Flatiron building, meekly sidestepping junkies and freaks. Their pent-up angst surfaced rather on home turf: under tables and amongst the legs of empire furniture, with an eye to the exposed ankle or shin of an old friend's shy lover or a nervous hanger-on—Maxime had quite a following. Any complaint was shamelessly met with full dragon treatment. Large accusing eyes, an expression of horror: "How dare you! What do you mean?" Culpability would invariably be precision-bombed straight back to the victim's feet, with a challenge to prompt apology.

Such bullying kept Maxime sharp and she was forgiven for being just as wonderful and entertaining as she was ghastly—and she was ghastly indeed. As a teenager I would turn up a couple of hours early when I could and help her land dinner. As she shuffled about wearing brightly varnished nails and clutching a clinking lipstick-stained glass of pastis, I would put on an apron, take stock of what was in the oven, set the table, and sharpen her knives.

At these times I would often think of my English grandfather, Patrick Bine Ogilvie, who was a pole-vaulter, a botanist, and a pilot. I would endeavor to imagine what counsel he might have offered. He was a very practical man. He'd toss his laundry to his mother from the cockpit of his plane as he flew back to base. He was a squadron leader in the Royal Air Force who flew many reconnaissance missions in Hurricanes stripped of their guns to allow extra fuel load and the mounting of cameras.

I never met him as he was killed in action at just thirty-three years old, shot down in 1944 while returning from a solo mission photographing enemy troop movements ahead of the Allied advance. Nevertheless, his playful spirit and courage in the face of the seemingly impossible have a strong presence within the family, as does a fascination with flying. To fly, one needs to cultivate an objective understanding of the quality of the airspace around you, to visualize and negotiate elements and obstacles three dimensionally, all whilst applied to an alert awareness of your destination and the ever changing quality of conditions ahead. In short to maintain a bird's eye view along with a sharp and clear super-objective. Much like cooking.

Group Captain Patrick Bine Ogilvie sitting on the wing of his reconnaissance Hurricane, 1944

Converging a dinner to table *chez Max* entailed navigating through rather dense social fog. Less perilous than anti-aircraft fire, granted, yet landing great platters in crystal candle light under the dragon's eye called for both precision and presence of mind.

She took the precaution wherever she lived to scrape together every last cent and install highly functional kitchens equipped to the hilt. Her philosophy was that if you like eating omelets, buy yourself a pan suited to the task and a stove with a gas flame of sufficient force to give you ninety seconds of joy each time you cook one. Satisfaction is thus attained from executing a task with precision and care—even before the first bite. Having the right tools for the job at hand empowers you to cook to the full extent of your skills. It gives you the confidence to give rein to your imagination and allows cooking to be informed and shaped by the senses.

I have made reference to the integrity and vitality of natural produce in the preceding pages, to the seduction tactics of ripe fruit, to the texture and flavor of food picked or caught and eaten instantly. August apples, two crisp bites and a mouthful of juice. Sea scallops sliced in half and eaten raw, still quivering on the plate, with the faintest season-ing of oil and salt. But how does one serve such fare to a room full of people? Well, the answer is you can't, not without sufficient organization. When I cook singlehandedly for private clients I can manage a dozen or so guests and deliver optimum standards and detail. Otherwise I need a team.

If I am working alone, and the numbers are greater, I am obliged to adjust the menu accordingly. Once there are a couple of dozen hungry folk at the table the aperture of choice, in terms of what to feed them, rapidly narrows. This may seem obvious, and yet it is where many condemn themselves to failure before they even begin. A dinner party for twelve incurs logistics quite unlike those of cooking for twenty, or indeed for four. A generous rib of beef cooked to perfection over charcoal will feed a handful of friends. If there are twice as many people it will either require a barbecue twice the size, or take you twice the time to achieve the same standard.

Don't sauté fillets for a dinner party unless the objective is to showcase your pan skills, which seems hardly appropriate. Choose instead a dish you can prepare in advance. Perhaps poach a large fish in an herb and floral water court bouillon and dress it upon a serving dish elegantly. There is always a solution. If you stay attuned to the season, the atmosphere, and number of guests, the appropriate menu will likely suggest itself.

Let us imagine dinner for half a dozen friends, something simple, say roast chicken. It is autumn, mid-autumn, somewhere past the equinox and before the first frost—the home straight for the nightshade family, before dying back and composting themselves to the ground. Mushrooms are abundant, brought forth by sun following rainfall. There are chestnuts, pears, and butternut squash, perhaps the last of the season's borlotti beans, a choice of potatoes for mashing, and sprigs of bolting rocket, late tomatoes, and shoots of lovage to serve as salad.

Pre-dinner cocktail finger food could consist of the season's last figs quartered and wrapped in thin shawls of prosciutto; a morsel of young cheese with honeycomb on a mouthful of crisp, tart apple. Oysters on the half shell nesting in salted ice garnished with muslin-wrapped lemons. We might start with a soup of tender young cauliflower and parsley; and finish with a chili-and-bay-spiced apple compote, garnished with sheep yogurt, berries, and chestnut honey.

Following dessert, perhaps a granita, served in a frozen glass to cleanse the palate, concocted of fresh pomegranate juice, spiked with a blush of Campari, a dilution of good rosé wine, and sparkling water. Then you might bring to the table bowls of grapes and walnuts with chilled apple or pear moonshine for all to share. And water, lots of water.

When you are engaged with the produce you are cooking and if you are organized, a dinner party can be straightforward to execute. Indeed if you really are organized, you will be joyfully free to improvise and change the menu as you go. If on the other hand you are raggedly trying to remember what comes next and where such and such is, the whole enterprise will be a stressful waste of time and energy. Find the joy! For the above menu, read Part Two. Real cooking is about the action of cooking food, not the aspiration to cooked food. The magic is in the doing.

RECIPES

FINGER FOOD & COCKTAILS

SEASONED & SPICED SOFT FRUIT

*

CRUDITÉS

*

QUAIL EGGS

*

DELICACIES ON EPHEMERAL TOAST

*

GARNISHED FOIE-GRAS

*

APPLES & PEARS, CHEESES & HONEYS

*

PLATEAU DE FRUITS DE MER

*

SEASON'S PLENTY

Cocktails

Cocktail shaking is an art, and just like the inner cook, the inner bartender needs to culture mind's eye and palette. Oftentimes, not unlike barbecuing, cocktail shaking is hijacked by the machos among us. Roughly they form two camps: cocktail bores that bang on about cocktails drunk in famous bars, all whilst storming blindly into recipes they have lifted from such places. And then those who, as the man of the house, carve the roast and shake the cocktails—*because they can!* All quite regardless as to whether they know what they are doing. This constitutes a great shame, for too much Campari is most definitely too much Campari. The task is to source, season, and compose ingredients in accordance to taste and occasion. Cognac is not just cognac, but rather a certain quality of cognac distilled from the wine of a certain *terroir*. Fruit juice is not just fruit juice, but rather a fresh and natural product, a concentrate, a purée, or an industrial equivalent.

A Bloody Mary, when composed of freshly made tomato juice, clam juice, and grated horseradish is a revelation. You might invest yourself even further, perhaps, and macerate horseradish in fine vodka, filter the resulting concoction, and hold it frozen in reserve. Wild strawberries and borage flowers freeze elegantly into ice cubes to garnish a glass. (Have children do this, it makes for a distracting game.) Just as with cookery, recipes easily lead you astray if you follow them without an eye to context. There are no absolute rules to composition: focus on combinations that work to great effect. Use what you have to hand and shake what you are in the mood for.

There is consensus among the great shakers as to what composes a checklist of kit necessary to executing cocktails. Chill your cocktail glasses. Use ice—lots of ice—and never use the same ice twice. Shake your shaker hard. Be sure not to overfill it or ice and alcohol will shower the room. A cocktail does not hang about. Harry Craddock, the legendary bartender of the London Savoy in the 1920s, deemed it should be served and drunk "quickly…while it's laughing at you."

Wine-based cocktails are equally civilized, yet lighter. Demonstratively mineral, crisp, dry white wine with the subtlest blush of Campari and garnished with fruit (a slice of white peach, crushed mint, and a borage flower). This makes a great sunset cocktail.

Wine

The discovery of natural wines rather puts the conventional alternative into the shade. This is not judgment, merely observation. Once you become accustomed to clean wines made from grapes grown in live soil and crafted by natural methods, you come to experience the pleasures and aftereffects of viticulture free of pesticides, fertilizer, and additives. No more Château Headache. Rather the wine in your glass is demonstrative of a particular grape variety, grown on a particular plot of land on a given year—terroir.

You only have to holiday in a commercial wine-growing region to get an idea of the degree to which winemaking has become an industrialized process dependent on pesticides and fungicides. And this all happens out in the open, in the vineyards, before grapes are even harvested. Further yeasts, enzymes, nutrients, tannins, and stabilizers play their part in the vinification and aging processes behind closed cellar doors. Wine is one of the few food industries not regulated by labeling laws.

"Natural wine" is a contentious term. No official body affords it accreditation. The term differs from an organic denomination largely insofar as organic viticulture warrants chemical manipulation in the winemaking process, whereas natural wines are made with the strict minimum of chemical and technological intervention from grape to bottle. Natural growers nurture biodiversity all whilst embracing and observing nature, rather than fighting to control it. "Organic" and "biodynamic" are the tools, "natural" the philosophy.

It is not a recent development. With the domestication of the grape vine, Persians, Sumerians, Egyptians, and Phoenicians all crushed and fermented grapes into natural wines. Perhaps it was the Romans that first applied specialized knowledge to winemaking, who started fiddling about in attempts to stabilize wines for scale production and its movement across Empire. As with most labels the whole business makes for contention and palaver. Natural produce is much harder to scale, and this troubles the marketing mind. Multinational companies can successfully scale outsourced, airfreighted, organic produce to a label-sensitized public. Natural wines, though, remain the realm of the independent producer.

Wine is convivial and contextual. A humble table wine can taste magnificent drunk in the region of its production, but perhaps does not always travel so well. If I am to drink several wines over an evening it is vastly preferable that they come from the same soil, made by the same hand. Grand Crus from the famous châteaux are endowed with an aura of aspirational refinement and are often exquisite. The wine trade is a speculator's game. Fortunes repeatedly exchange hands over bottles that cross continents and are never opened. In my Harry's Bar days I would sometimes take liquid elevenses at a farmhouse in Italy, and the very same day fly back to London and open bottles of fancy vintages from the Annabel's wine cellar for swanky dinners. Fancy does not necessarily make for better. Nowadays I select and sell wines from independent biodynamic producers. As a cook I have a good view of the effect that wine has upon people. My advice is to play it natural. Fermented pesticides do not bring the best out in any of us.

Finger Food

Finger food, as its name suggests, is negotiated with one hand whilst holding a glass in the other and making conversation. It is the evanescent quality and jewel-like proportions of *amuse-gueules* that hold charm. A bite of something delicious that leaves you in anticipation for more. All with an ear to conversation, as you inwardly rack your brain for the name of the person engaging you. And sip a well-shaken cocktail, furtively casting an eye across the room for a familiar face. Longing to be saved by choice and plenty. By a tray of white peach doused in olive oil, grappa, and salt. A mouthful of cardamom melon, a Javanese-peppered strawberry, a dice of raw sea scallop nesting upon a sliver of iced radish. As a rule, finger food is pretty foul, prepared drastically in advance and refrigerated. At a cocktail party one learns to deliver a polite, yet curt "thank you but no thank you" to servile tray bearers. It needn't be so.

Dare to serve a banquet of elegant delicacies on flying platters. Your guests will be enchanted. The key is to thoroughly prepare all the component parts in advance and assemble them at the very last minute. Finger food is ephemeral, convivial, and inclusive. It should jump at the eye. An ounce or two of caviar goes a long way as garnish. Four dozen quail eggs, laddered to vertiginous heights of hospitality. Compose your menu in harmony with the cocktail or wines to be served. I favor textured, clean, and savory over sweet—ephemeral finger food, to stimulate the palate and open the appetite.

Let Us Not Forget the Children

I love to cook. It provides sustenance, conviviality, and a living to me, and foremost offers an environment in which intuition and instinct operate freely. This I imagine comes from my conditioning as a young child, having been brought up among cooks and gardeners, cooking and gardening. Curious, playful children make dependable *commis-chefs*.

It is not complicated to assemble cucumber and cheese, put the candles in a birthday cake, or swim a fish around a sink full of water. And such distractions start the ball rolling. What can I do next, they ask? Well, you can make a salad dressing. Weigh the flour. Separate the yolks from the whites. Why don't you go and get your stool so you can reach? This is your whisk and your bowl. Now, it's yours, look after it, wash it up and put it away. Go and pick me some parsley, please. Get such and such from the larder. They soon learn the ropes.

Involving kids in kitchen tasks and granting them the opportunity to see simple jobs through from start to finish builds confidence and develops autonomy. It allows them to use their intuition and senses. There is no glamour in grownups eating a refined menu at one table, whilst the children are being fed crap next door by a nanny. Better by far to eat together; children are naturally curious—endeavor to culture their senses.

Sharing

Generosity and equality have a way of emerging at table. A bowl of walnuts at the end of an autumn supper. A glut of asparagus on a huge serving plate—white, green, and wild for all to share—with an abundance of tarragon mayonnaise. Great towering mountains of crushed ice garnished with oysters, crab claws, whelks, and barnacles. Such fare serves to focus moderation, etiquette, and gallantry into a maelstrom of sharing. In such a context, greed and bad manners are exposed in an instant. Eating together has a civilizing effect. Sharing food from the same bowl instills a sense of equality and communion to a meal. It is nigh on impossible to both fight and eat at once.

Seasoned & Spiced Soft Fruit

The peach and nectarine season here extends from mid-June until mid-September. There exist a wealth of varieties (heirloom to hybrid), of flavors (sweet to tart), and colors (white to yellow to pink to violet). The peach originates from the Kunlun Mountains in northwest China from where it gradually made its way west via India to the Near East, before hitching a ride with Alexander the Great to Europe. Yellow peaches are sweeter than their white cousins, and as such generally a hit with children.

Peaches and nectarines ripen on the branch. Just as melons, peaches require the umbilical connection to the starches of the mother to fully ripen. If picked green they will never develop the sugars necessary to achieve full potential of flavor. Again, scale of production has great import upon the vitality of the fruit tendered for sale. An independent producer will harvest daily for local markets. An industrial-scale producer will harvest green fruit for shipment and wholesale. The resultant disparity in texture and flavor stands tall.

During peach season, if you are able to procure delicate, pert, ripe specimens, seize the moment. A mouthful of lively and tart peeled white peach is delectably enhanced when seasoned with a pinch of fleur de sel, a drop of extra virgin olive oil, and a splash of grappa. The eye registers the peach and then as you bite it, oil, salt, and grappa ambush the palate. The contrast results in peach tasting surprisingly more of peach than it ever does alone. Served in regimented lines upon polished flying platters these make for winning finger food.

I serve seasoned soft fruit throughout the summer months as palate openers. It is enough to imagine a combination of flavors that appeal. And though this is to a degree subjective, there are a host of universal natural synergies that suggest themselves. Strawberries with Javanese pepper for instance, or Charentais melon with cardamom to name but two.

Dragonetta Cocktail

Select pomegranates of dark complexion that when tapped with the back of the knuckle, ring a hollow sound, these oftentimes yield the best juice. Slice the pomegranate around the waist exposing the seeds within; the brighter the color the better. Remove the seeds, taking care to discard bitter pith, and with a ladle to hand pass these gently through a fine sieve to extract their juice. Pass this once more through muslin to obtain a clear ruby colored liquid. Perform this task as close to the hour of serving as possible. It will not keep. The color unforgivingly betrays the barman who works too far in advance.

In a cocktail shaker garnished with ice, add three parts rosé wine, one part freshly squeezed pomegranate juice, and the faintest blush of Campari. Shake the cocktail awake and then top it up with one part sparkling water. Garnish chilled stemmed glasses and serve. A light and refreshing summer cocktail that can be drunk in quantities all whilst remaining relatively sober.

Crudités For the Children

In a cocktail environment, children, if they are to be seen and indeed heard, should be catered for. Even encouraged to help with preparations. Raw vegetables—cucumbers and carrots, celery, crisply textured baby zucchini with their beheaded flowers, segments of Florence fennel cut like chocolate orange, and other such raw nutritious fare—will distract and placate young souls, helping them feel part, *and party*. And if joining in is to be done properly, the kids need a cocktail too.

Serendipity Junior   Crushed mint on ice with apple juice, topped up with sparkling water.

And for the Grownups

When serving flying platters of crudités, a practical solution is to prepare vegetable *Gunkan* sushi. Using a mandoline, thinly shave radish, zucchini, or indeed fruit. If you have a meat slicer or surplus patience and the sleight of hand for the aforementioned prosciutto knife, mangoes, papayas, peaches, apples, and pears are all suitable. As are indeed cold meats—leftover roast belly of pork cut paper thin and rolled around apple, rocket, and mint, spiked with chutney to delight the unsuspecting palate with umami. This is a good general tactic to employ with finger food: do not show your whole hand. Deceive the eye so as to ambush the palate.

Detail the slivers of vegetable, fruit, or meat into rolling-paper-shaped rectangular lengths. Square off the bottoms and reserve under damp muslin whilst you prepare the garnish.

Assemble matchstick-shaped *batonets* of carrots and celery, fennel, tomato, artichoke heart, whatever scraps you have to hand. Garnish and roll your *gunkan*, pinning them together with a cocktail stick. Compose contrasting textures and flavors that celebrate natural synergies.

Make a mayonnaise spiced to your taste (see page 82). Detail a serving tray with equally spaced drops of mayonnaise. Garnish these with the *gunkan* in neat soldierly lines, all seasoned standing to attention firmly footed in their sauce.

Serendipity Cocktail   Calvados on ice with crushed mint and borage, topped up with champagne.

Quail Eggs

The nutritional and medicinal properties of quails' eggs have been championed in the East since antiquity. They are said to contain a much higher proportion of both minerals and vitamins than are found in hens' eggs. Yet, an egg is only really as good as the diet of the bird that lays it. I have a neighbor who keeps quails, bantams, ducks, and geese. We all do, if we seek them out.

Lovage is a perennial herb that puts up new shoots in early April. It bolts, goes to flower, and on to seed from the month of June. *Levisticum officinale* is an herbaceous perennial that grows rapidly to impressive height, easily six foot, so you want to plant it at the back of a border or where the shadow it casts will not obstruct. The young leaves are a key component of a spring herb salad, though the older leaves overwhelm the palate.

The rootstock is eaten as a vegetable and has medicinal qualities: as a carminative, a diuretic, and a stomachic. Old wives tell that lovage promotes the onset of menstruation, and so should be given wide berth by the pregnant. The flower, which becomes the seeds, is what I am referring to in this recipe; I use them as a spice, to season salt.

Fleur de sel, literally translated, means flower of salt. It is labor intensive to produce and thus expensive. Nevertheless it is quite the subtlest of all seasoning salts. It consists of the first crystals that form at the surface of saltpans. These are hand raked and carefully collected before they fall back below the surface of the water. Fleur de sel is not for cooking; it is for seasoning food just before it hits the table. It is a relatively humid salt and so does not immediately dissolve when used to season soups or sauces. It retains its irregularly sized crystal structure and consequently dissolves at different rates in the mouth bringing textured phases of seasoning to a dish.

Control of temperature is the key to perfect boiled eggs. If the temperature stays too high for too long the eggs quickly turn to sulfur bullets. Eggshells are porous, so you can qualify eggs as they come to a simmer by adding herbs or herb-flavored vinegars to the cooking water. For quails' eggs, I add a splash of tarragon-flavored rice vinegar. Place eggs into a pan and cover with cold water. Bring the water steadily up to a simmer over a low flame and the moment you see air bubbles rising from the bottom of the pan to the surface, turn off the heat.

For a soft-boiled quail egg, count to ninety before fishing it out and banging it on the head to allow the heat to escape and arrest the cooking. For a hard-boiled egg, one where the yolk has just set, three minutes should suffice. If it is not set enough for your taste leave the eggs in the pan a little longer. They will gently continue to cook in the accumulated temperature of the water. And the operative word here is *gently*, for as the pan is off the heat, no sulfur disaster can occur.

It is a method of cooking I employ often. That is, allowing things to rest to perfection in their accumulated temperature. With instinct, trial, and error, you learn to judge the moment that a dish is under-cooked to perfection—the precise moment to rescue it from the heat source, so as to let it rest, to doneness.

Assemble the lovage salt by finely chopping the lovage seeds together with fleur de sel. You might do this in a mortar and pestle. The proportion should be judged to your palate and to the quality of the lovage. From fragrant fresh flowers to the much stronger flavor of dry seeds that in the depths of winter you might keep sealed airtight in a jar in the larder.

Quails' eggs seasoned just so make for timelessly elegant finger food. Topped with caviar as a double egg hit, they're not bad either.

A Bicycle   Garnish chilled wine glasses with a sprig of mint, a generous slice of white peach, wild strawberries, and a borage leaf; cover this with a lid of ice. Add a blush of Campari and then top up with chilled dry white wine. Light wines with a hint of effervescence to them work well. Garnish with a borage flower. It is called a bicycle because once you are on, you are on, just keep pedaling, have another.

Delicacies on Ephemeral Toast

Ephemeral toast is best made from paper-thin slivers of good spelt or sourdough bread that are dried to crisp in a low oven. One textured bite. Garnished with a delicacy.

Crabmeat bejeweled in its coral. The peeled flesh of an heirloom tomato seasoned with flowering basil. Foie gras with the fresh spice of a crushed green coriander seed. Any delectable scrap served upon a bite of ephemeral toast.

Cut the bread with a prosciutto knife. The thin and flexible long blade allows precise control over its center of gravity, thus enabling paper-thin slicing. If you have one, use a meat slicer with the blade set to number two.

Detail the slices of bread into mouth-sized pieces. Place them on a tray in an oven set to 175°F (80°C) and keep a sharp eye on progress. The whole process will take no more than five minutes. The objective is to have the toast crisp without changing color. Any color would infer singeing and, by association, unpalatable bitterness. Aim to catch the precise moment the bread is purged of all humidity and so just crisp.

Often, for less formal occasions, I toast the slices whole and break them by hand as they come out of the oven. This makes for an eclectic mix of shapes, and is very pretty, if somewhat wasteful. If you are receiving a large number of guests, simplify things and organize a counted reserve of even, bite-size pieces that you can tray up easily into regiments.

Natural dry rosé wine perfectly chilled

When serving rich garnished finger food from late spring to autumn, dry rosé wine makes the perfect accompaniment. Look for rosé that is pale in color and demonstratively mineral.

Garnished Foie Gras

Late October, and the wind is blowing from the north. This evening, as I walked up from the lake through the wood toward a rising moon, a familiar distant-beaked chatter caught my attention from above: a magnificent orderly V-shaped formation of geese heading west against the dusk sky.

It brings foie gras to mind. These geese have been stuffing their crops to bursting point on cereals ahead of their migratory flight home. The Egyptians would stalk and ensnare migratory wild geese so as to feast on their pre-flight livers. Seems *less-worse* somehow than imprisoned force-feeding. The thought of commercial foie gras is unappetizing in the extreme, just as is that of cage-farmed fish.

Quality foie gras of goose or duck is, however, a delicacy. Ducks and geese need water and space. At the Bailey they would put their beaks to the stream and in a swaying motion hoover freshwater shrimp up their long necks. Much waddling and bathing went on, preening and depositing of nitrogen in their wake, ever in loud pursuit of pasture and slugs.

Once you have foie gras sourced, it is the so-called *mi-cuit* (half-cooked) variety to go for. It is cooked to a lower heart temperature and thereby retains more of the liver's delicate texture and natural flavor. It has a much shorter shelf life than mass-produced pasteurized foie gras, so again, look to independent producers.

Depending on the occasion and the number of people to feed, you might serve this upon trays, elegant little mouthfuls on ephemeral toast. However, when numbers permit, for occasions informal, simply bring a whole lobe of foie gras to the kitchen table. Grill a mountain of toast; bring a bottle of olive oil and a cellar of fleur de sel for all to reach. Organize a bowl of herbs, their leaves, flowers, and green seeds.

Johnny Applejack   Garnish an iced shaker with crushed mint, applejack, apple juice, grated ginger, and a squeeze of lime. Shake it awake. Serve in a chilled tumbler on the rocks with a sliver of lime and a twist of mint.

Apples & Pears, Cheeses & Honeys

Scrumping in an August orchard, filling one's pockets to bursting; two crisp bites of an apple, a mouth full of juice, instant gratification. You will likely bite into half a dozen or so, and satiated, leave it that. If they were cookies you might finish the packet and still crave more.

Orchard fruit comes all at once, in a glut. August and September is for apples and pears. As soon as I bite them, my palate anticipates the subtle, salty, crumbling texture of pecorino cheese. It is a harvest picnic: cheese in one hand and apple in the other. By this time of year the cheeses made from the milk of flower-rich spring pasture are four to six months old. Maturing, deepening in flavor, hardening in texture. Then there is the cheese, barely a week old, that follows you throughout the year, ever young, ephemeral, and clean.

Tart apple and mildly salty cheese—simplicity heaven-sent—garnished with honey. Honey of the flowers of heather, wild thyme, or common bramble for an autumnal feel. Acacia or rosemary-flower honey to evoke spring and regeneration.

Well-stored apples keep from harvest until May. It is a question of temperature and hydration. So either side of summer peach season, you can serve this all year-round.

Vin de Voile

Vin Jaune or Vin de Voile is wine that is ever so slightly oxidized. It is matured in oak barrels, nurtured under a naturally forming raft-like film of yeasts over a period of six years.

Considerable evaporation occurs and to reference this "angel's share" the wine is bottled in measures of 620ml (20 oz). It is a quality of wine well suited to cheese. In fact, it is preferable to red. The tannins of young, and especially oaked, red wines easily overpower the palate and prevent the appreciation of the full flavor of cheeses. A lightly oxidized white, or Vin de Voile, underscores and enhances the subtle meadow-flower flavors of natural cheeses.

Plateau de Fruits de Mer

Half a dozen oysters and a fist full of clams: to eat raw with a muslin-wrapped lemon in the other hand. Sea scallops, opened and eaten without delay, seasoned with a pinch of fleur de sel and the faintest dash of olive oil. One controlled action with a sharp knife will slice a live scallop in two, making for generous sashimi.

Grey shrimp, lobster, barnacles, crabs, and whelks poached with delicate precision. Served with elegant slivers of spelt bread and freshly whisked mayonnaise. Cover the whelks in cold water, bring them up to a boil once, then discard the water and start again. For the third time, bring the whelks up to barely a simmer, and simmer them thus in a court bouillon of your concoction for a quarter of an hour. Then turn off the heat and allow the whelks to cool in their broth. Composed of a bay leaf, a sprig of parsley, the flesh of a mild chili, a hint of ginger: a court bouillon seasoned and spiced, according to mood and occasion.

To poach crab and lobster is an exercise so simple that it almost takes care of itself. The succulence and essence of their flavor is to be found within the protein of their flesh, and so the key lies in proceeding delicately. Just as chlorophyll oxidizes above a certain temperature and greens turn grey, protein—once abandoned to too high a temperature—is purged from flesh and rapidly becomes the grey-white mass of foam or scum one only too often sees floating upon the surface of a cauldron that boils furiously. To poach is to poach, not to boil.

To emulate seawater, bring a generous-sized pan of water salted to two tablespoons per quart (thirty-five grams per liter) to a rolling boil. Plunge in the live crab or lobster, close the lid, and turn off the flame. Poach at 175°F (80°C), counting roughly ten minutes per pound, (twenty minutes per kilogram). And that is it: rich Atlantic flavors that in very few gestures come to grace your table.

Mayonnaise

All that remains to be done is to rustle up a mayonnaise. Bring to room temperature an egg yolk of known provenance, a coffee spoon of mustard, and enough olive oil to make the volume you require. With positive spirit and elbow grease, whisk these into an emulsion. First combine the mustard together with yolk, and then add the oil in a steady flow. With care, one yolk will easily bind a pint of oil; if you desire a richer result use more yolks. There are no rules, only a turn of hand that you will acquire with time.

Open the oysters; good fishmongers will do this if asked. It is not difficult. It just requires the right knife. Take a cloth in your left hand in which to hold the oyster immobile. If you slip you will easily stab yourself, so do this properly. With the tip of the oyster knife, burrow towards the adductor muscle, twist for leverage, and once the blade is under the shell, sever the muscle exposing the oyster within. Remember to open a bottle of Sancerre . . . et voilà a feast upon a mountain of ice.

Season's Plenty

Finger food has just as much place at table as it does at cocktail hour. Seasonal gluts are an opportunity to glean sensorial reference from a given ingredient at the top of its game, for feast and celebration, for the sharing of plenty and giving of thanks. A season's simple abundance, served as it comes, with the very minimum of transformation, straight to table.

It might be a medley of asparagus—green, white, and wild—to celebrate the month of April. Whatever it may be, the key lies in immediacy, in eating asparagus that have been picked and within minutes cooked. Asparagus this fresh require almost no more than leaving well alone. Green ones are preferable eaten raw as crudité, picked from their bed and bitten upon with a sprig of neighboring tarragon. White asparagus have a more pronounced and bitter flavor and the skin is more fibrous. The solution: to peel the asparagus thoroughly before cooking. If you have a reflex to hold back, because you feel extravagant or wasteful, you have got the wrong end of the stick.

Peelings, the coarser ends of the spears, and mineral water are all quickly transformed into broth. This, in turn, becomes the heart of a risotto. There need be no waste in a resourceful kitchen. Skip false economy and peel the spears of all fibrous coarseness. Guests unable to bite or chew these would only leave them gnawed and gnarled at the sides of their plates. It is a good rule of thumb for preparation: organize vegetables ahead of cooking as you wish to serve them. Prep it, blanch it, and eat it. Delectable leftovers can always be recycled.

A mountain of corn on the cob for a hungry table of children that have been running around swimming and biking—this makes a perfect menu for dinner outside under a falling summer sun. Briskly boiled to tender, served with olive oil and fleur de sel (or butter if it is good). Skewer both ends like handlebars, corn to cunningly loosen wobbly teeth. A high tea or lunch for children could be artichokes simmered or steamed, served with vinaigrette, in which to dip the leaves. A fork slid under the edge of your plate, so as to slant it, into a trough, for dipping. The undressing of an artichoke has a great sense of closure to it. Down to the delicate removal of the choke that reveals the heart.

My favorites by far are the baby ones, stripped down and eaten raw. Dipped in oil and salt, they make for perfect elevenses. On a spring morning after a couple hours of work, quarters of young, tender, purple artichoke seasoned thus, eaten with sprigs of parsley and chased down with half a glass of watered-down wine. Greengages, damsons, fresh almonds, hazelnuts, walnuts, cherries, and apricots: these might grace a table at the end of a meal. Bowls brought forth, to pick upon whilst chatting, perhaps partaking in moonshine, lengthening the day and generally staying up. From dawn to elevenses, through high tea to dinner and beyond, seasonal gluts converged to table inspire souls to share.

SOUPS & BROTHS

CARROT & TARRAGON

∗

CAULIFLOWER & PARSLEY

∗

LENTIL, GARLIC & ROSEMARY

∗

LIGHT CHICKEN BROTH, GINGER & CHILI

∗

ROCKFISH BROTH, SAFFRON & OYSTERS

∗

POT-AU-FEU

∗

CHILLED MELON & CARDAMOM

Soup

In *cucina povera* (rural peasant cooking), bread garnishes a bowl, and a ladle of soup from an ever-simmering cauldron is poured upon it. This timeless action is embodied in the word that soup is derived from, the Latin *suppare*, to soak. As in broth poured onto bread, providing a nutritious and sustaining meal.

Indeed the French peasant term for any meal is *la soupe. C'est l'heure de la soupe.* You don't dine, you soup! *Allons souper*, the Pre–Marshall Plan Gang will chime, by way of invitation to table.

Soup has been with us since the dawn of cooking and has comforting, identity-reinforcing character. Geography, season, and circumstance are expressed in the ingredients used to compose a soup. It projects identity from southern to northern and from noble to rustic. The key to making soup is organizing your ingredients in such a way that they require the absolute minimum amount of cooking time. The idea is to source the freshest of raw ingredients and to celebrate their flavors and the natural synergies that occur between them. Think a branch of tarragon for carrots, bolting parsley for cauliflower, sage for pumpkin, rosemary for lentils.

An Asian mandoline vegetable slicer with an adjustable blade allows you to cut vegetables to a regulated thickness. It makes the task of preparing vegetables for soup much easier; however, exercise caution: a mandoline will slice fingers as efficiently as it slices vegetables.

To make soup: firstly mandoline your ingredients to paper-thin. In a cast iron or heavy copper-based pan, toast them in herb-infused fat until translucent. Then deglaze the pan with broth and bring its contents to a simmer. Test for salt, add an abundance of the relevant herb on the branch, close the lid, and turn off the heat. Stand the pan to infuse. It will gently continue cooking in its accumulated temperature. Leave well alone for twenty minutes or so whilst the herbs and vegetables infuse the broth. Then remove the herbs and transfer the soup to a blender. Pulse-pulverize the mixture, adding olive oil for body and texture.

Reheat if necessary, taking care not to oxidize any green herbs that may have been added to specific recipes. Take extreme care with temperature or all your efforts will have been in vain, for chlorophyll taken over 145°F (63°C) oxidizes—greens turn to grey and delicate flavors to bitter tastes.

There is a reflex—largely Anglo-Saxon—to serve soup blisteringly hot. I always keep in mind that flavor is so much more alive at a slightly cooler temperature. Try the experiment yourself: eat the same thing cold, warm, and then very hot. The reflex will be to adjust the seasoning each time despite the fact that the dish remains the same and only the temperature varies.

Soffritto

A soffritto serves to impart a fragrant base flavor to soups, sauces, and stews and can be composed of pretty much anything, though classically the key ingredients will be onion, leek, celery, and carrot, all chopped into a fine, even-sized dice (a mirepoix) no larger than the main ingredient to follow. The word soffritto comes from the Italian verb *soffrigere*, which means "to gently fry." The logic is as follows: firstly, with a mandoline, organize a vegetable into slices of even thickness. With a sharp knife, cut these slices into julienne (squared-edged lengths), and then proceed to chop the julienne into a mirepoix. If you bruise a vegetable as you chop, it will bleed, and texture will be irreversibly lost. One controlled action that cuts cleanly through the vegetable fibers is the answer. Learn how to use a knife and keep it sharp. Whilst peeling, chopping, and carefully using a mandoline, you will accumulate a quantity of tops, roots, peelings, and offcuts that you'll discard from your mirepoix. Endeavor to be ruthless, as all these bits can rise again as broth.

To qualify the base flavor of a soffritto, oftentimes I add a whole branch of a given herb that enjoys a synergy with the main ingredient, so as to be able to then remove the branch, with ease, once the herb has imparted the best of its flavor (and perhaps replace it afresh, until the aperture of flavor is set). Add chili, bay, lemongrass, or whatever you aspire to taste. Indeed you may even omit the soffritto entirely and focus on infusing the cooking fats with generous branches of the accompanying herbs. There is no rule, only what circumstance, season, and hunger inspire in you.

Chicken Broth

The golden rule to making good broth is *never boil*. The standard proportion of liquid to matter is equal parts: one to one. Simmer to desired taste, stand to rest, then strain and store for future use. Oftentimes people will boil up the carcass of a roast chicken. This makes stock not broth. For vegetable soups one wants fragrant and delicate broths. For chicken broth an easy and rapid way to make progress is to source chicken thighs, skin them, cover them in mineral water, and bring them to a simmer, clearing the surface as you go until it runs clear. Continue to simmer gently until the desired flavor is attained.

Fish Broth

For those who live by the sea and have easy access to an abundance of fresh fish at dockside prices, there is no shortage of cheaper specimen with which to make light fragrant broths. In a city you need to make friends with a fishmonger. A lot of the fish you see on the counter will be prepared as fillets. This oftentimes means that there are nutritious bones backstage, to be bought relatively inexpensively. It is always worth asking. You may just walk out with a bag full of this morning's sole, sea bass, and turbot bones. It is worth noting that salmon, mackerel, sardine, anchovy, and other such oily fish are to be avoided when it comes to making broth. If you do try, your nose will swiftly warn your palate away. Such leftovers are much better marinated, seasoned, and spiced, then grilled and gnawed at in the privacy of the kitchen in the manner of hungry cats.

A delicate and inexpensive broth can be made with the small rockfish that go into a bouillabaisse. As with all fish broth, the key here is in meticulous cleaning. Invest in a good pair of scissors for removing gills and fins. Thoroughly clean all trace of the intestine that runs along the roof of the stomach cavity. Then remove the gills and the eyes; if left in, they will cloud your broth. Whether you are working with a whole specimen or just bones, roughly chop the fish up to increase the gelatinous quality of the broth by exposing bone to water.

When cooking crab or lobster, save the skulls for making broth. A clear lobster or crab broth garnished with a morsel of remaining meat makes for a refined dish of recycled leftovers. Every part of these creatures finds a role in the kitchen apart from the lungs, or "dead lady's fingers" as they are rather sinisterly called. These run alongside the skull and should be removed with a sharp pair of scissors. This done, bash up the skull with the back of a rolling pin and then, as above, *never boil*. The standard proportion of liquid to matter is equal parts one to one. Simmer to desired taste, stand to rest; then strain and store for future use.

Dashi

Dashi is the base broth at the heart of much Japanese cookery. A dashi will enhance and harmonize the flavors of other ingredients. It is a delicate and fragrant broth—when made with care—imparting irresistible background umami to any dish, sauce, or soup. To make one: take kombu (kelp seaweed) and wipe it clean with damp muslin. Put this into a small saucepan and cover it generously with mineral water. Bring the pan to just under a boil, then take it off the heat and add a handful of dried shaved bonito flakes. Stand this to infuse until the desired depth of flavor is achieved. Then strain the dashi broth through muslin, and that's it.

Vegetable Broth

I think of vegetable broth in two forms. Firstly, there is general vegetable broth that every resourceful cook using fresh ingredients can easily conjure. This is composed of peelings, tops, roots, and offcuts that, whilst too noble for the compost bucket, do not quite make it to table. Such a broth is suitable for stews, pulses, and hearty soups. Secondly, there are vegetable broths that are delicate, fragrant, and composed of tops, roots, and peelings specific to the soup in question. These broths I like to prepare as one would a tisane. For carrot and tarragon, think leek tops, carrots, and an onion. Bring this gently up to a simmer and then, as with a tisane, turn off the heat and stand the concoction to infuse—slipping in a bay leaf, the flesh of a mild chili, and a generous branch of tarragon before covering with a lid.

Carrot & Tarragon

The best carrots are to be had from spring till autumn. Tarragon is at its best in early summer. Carrots are crisp in texture, sweet in taste, and packed with carotene that the body converts into vitamin A to promote our immune system. To lift a carrot from healthy soil, rinse it under a garden tap, and then eat it with a sprig of tarragon is a simple luxury that, given half a chance, kids will embrace gleefully. Right up to nibbling the faintly bitter stem of the green top and the gentle crunch and aftertaste of soil. The vitality of their green tops will communicate to the eye a pretty clear idea of how long they have been out of the ground.

Tarragon is a perennial plant that lies dormant in the winter to push up new tender shoots in spring. Whilst the plant is dormant you can split, divide, and multiply the rootstock to plant in new soil. Its timing is impeccable as it emerges from the ground together with the first asparagus—it is hard to find a finer pairing between vegetable and herb. To cut an asparagus spear from its bed and eat it instantly with a new tender shoot of tarragon is to savor the month of April.

INGREDIENTS
—*Serves 6*

A bunch of carrots, 2lbs (1kg)
A leek
Olive oil
A knob of butter
Bay leaves
A branch of tarragon
Fleur de sel, to taste
5 cups (1.2l) chicken broth

Mandoline and finely chop the carrots. Finely chop the leek. Set aside. Heat a pan and add olive oil and a knob of butter. Oil has a much higher threshold for heat than butter, and therefore should always enter the pan first. Add bay leaves and a generous branch of tarragon to infuse the fats.

Raise the flame to medium high, add the carrots and leek to the pan and sauté them briefly, impregnating them thus with tarragon flavored fats. As you have organized both leek and carrot into paper-thin dice, they require virtually no cooking. Remove the tarragon before it oxidizes, and taste and season for salt. Now deglaze the pan with a little of the chicken broth, working the fat and broth into an emulsion containing the essence extracted from the vegetables. Then add the remaining broth to cover the carrot and leek mixture. Use less broth for a thicker soup and vice versa. Again, taste and season. Bring the soup up to a rolling simmer and add another generous branch of tarragon. Cover with a lid and turn off the flame.

Let it stand covered to rest, allowing it to gently cook and infuse in the accumulated temperature. Resist the temptation to lift the lid for a good twenty minutes. Then remove the tarragon and taste. When satisfied with the flavor, blend it, adding olive oil for body and texture.

Carefully reheat the soup and ladle it into hot bowls garnished with sprigs of bolting tarragon and a dash of extra virgin olive oil. Serve immediately.

Cauliflower & Parsley

Once the evening temperatures begin to drop in early autumn and there's been rain and a waxing moon, parsley, leeks, and cauliflower all begin to perk up and catch the eye. I find smaller, younger cauliflowers to be better textured and of finer flavor.

Cauliflower has a rich and distinct flavor, so I often make this soup with mineral water. As a first course served for city folk at dinner, mineral water is preferable, as it will subtly showcase the delicate flavors of parsley, leek, cauliflower, and bay, all whilst stimulating the appetite. An autumn supper after a physical day, however, calls for chicken broth—to nourish, strengthen, and satiate with umami. As always, it depends what you have done, and or whom you are feeding.

Alternatively, a light vegetable broth can be assembled. Make an infusion using the leftover green leek tops, its meticulously cleansed root, and parsley stalks. Add a sprig of bay and a hint of chili if you wish. Gently bring this to a simmer in mineral water and then stand to infuse before straining and reserving for use.

Parsley invigorates the palette and complements an array of ingredients from potatoes to anchovies, garlic to artichokes, shellfish to bone marrow, and on and on. I love parsley and would choose it as a desert island luxury. Parsley is native to southeastern Europe and western Asia and is a frost-hardy biennial that grows very easily. If you plant a row and cover it through the winter you will enjoy a constant supply. There is curly parsley (think English butcher counters), and then there is flat-leaf parsley, which has a more pronounced flavor.

I sow parsley at staggered intervals to have a constant supply at different stages of maturity over the course of the year. If you keep cutting the plant back, new tender shoots emerge over and over again well into a second year and beyond. When it bolts and goes to flower, I use the seeds as a fresh spice for seasoning. As with other delicate herbs, it is a joy to have young tender leaves, bolting sprigs, flowers, and young green seeds of the same variety all at hand at once, so as to savor the sensory arc from fragrant leaf to fresh spice. The key to successfully making this soup is paying attention to temperature. Boiling the cauliflower will quickly result in sulfur broth. If you then proceed to carelessly boil and oxidize the parsley you will create grey and bitter sulfur broth.

INGREDIENTS —Serves 6

A head of cauliflower
A leek
A bunch of parsley
Extra virgin olive oil
A knob of butter
Bay leaves, to taste
A mild chili
5 cups (1.2l) broth, or mineral water
Fleur de sel, to taste

Mandoline and finely chop a cauliflower. Finely chop the leek: first remove the green tops and root that you might use to infuse your broth. Cut the white leek stem in half along the vertical. Divide each half in two, by removing the center. Now detail each rectangular quarter of leek into julienne, and then dice these into a mirepoix.

Heat a pan; add olive oil and a knob of butter. Add bay, parsley stalks, and chili to infuse the fats. Add the cauliflower and then the leek. Gently toast until translucent, and then remove the herbs.

Deglaze the pan with a little of the chosen broth, working the fat and the broth into an emulsion containing the essence extracted from the vegetables.

Add the remaining broth (less for a thicker soup and vice versa). Taste and season for salt, and bring the soup up to a rolling simmer; add the stalks from your bunch of parsley, a couple of bay leaves, and the deseeded flesh of a mild chili. Cover with a lid and turn off the flame. Let it stand covered to rest, allowing it to gently cook and infuse in the accumulated temperature. Resist the temptation to lift the lid for a good twenty minutes. Then remove the herbs, wringing them for all they yield. To avoid splashing, firstly spoon the vegetables into the blender, and then pour in the broth. Pulse blend to desired consistency.

If you wish to serve the soup piping hot, it is now, before the addition of the parsley leaves, that you should return it to the pan and bring it back up to temperature. Then return the heated soup to the blender and add abundant parsley.

It is the subtle flavor of parsley that one aspires to, so, in addition to leaf and tender stems, reach for bolting sprigs and young flowers if you can. To finish the soup, incorporate olive oil into the blender for body and texture. Taste and correct the seasoning. Before serving, make sure that everybody is at table. Garnish heated soup plates with parsley flowers, a line of olive oil, and then pour over the soup.

Lentil, Garlic & Rosemary

This is a hearty soup for autumn and winter. Throughout early autumn, garnish it with summer garlic before it begins to shoot. In Italy and France there is a tradition of eating lentils on New Year's Day, it is said to bring prosperity for the year ahead. So if you live among Mediterraneans, you might well stock your larder in advance.

I have a neighbor, an elderly and most elegant peasant gentleman whose family has farmed garlic and the prized Le Puy lentil for generations. Lentils cultivated in live soil by natural method can be found and are an inexpensive and nutritious asset to any larder. Lentils have been farmed since the dawn of agriculture. They are cooked in a multitude of ways the world over and provide a staple source of protein. There are two general types: flat, broad, and light-colored ones that rapidly turn to mush, and then the rounder, small and greenish-black ones that I refer to in this recipe. These, gently simmered and cooked with care, hold their shape and texture well.

Garlic, *Allium sativum*, is a member of the onion family, as are leeks and chives. It is the shoot or the germ of mature garlic that is hard to digest and that causes foul garlic breath. Young freshly harvested garlic is almost sweet, and early in the season requires no more than blanching or steaming for a minute or two. As the season progresses this will become a minute or three, and so on up until the moment when you will be halving the garlic to remove the young forming shoot and perhaps weighing up whether to use garlic at all.

An emblem of remembrance and fidelity and championed by old wives as a tonic to memory, rosemary is native to the arid chalk hills of the Mediterranean. *Rosmarinus officinalis* will survive on little more than humidity carried in on the sea breeze. A member of the mint family *Lamiaceae*, the name derives from the Latin *ros* for dew and *marinus* for sea—dew of the sea, which references the plant's hardiness.

Often people talk up the merits of dried rosemary. I am not a fan of dried herbs in general; they tend to verge toward bitterness, with the possible exception of oregano, or lime flowers and verbena for tisane. I prefer to harvest herbs at the peak of their flavor and macerate them in olive oil or vinegar, so as to have them in the larder bottled, corked, and within reach throughout the year. Rosemary, to the great delight of the honeybee, is an evergreen that flowers in early spring ahead of orchards. Its fragrant branches of green leaves can be harvested year-round. It has a rich, oily, and faintly woody floral scent that is exquisite. So when working with rosemary I will briefly introduce a fresh branch at progressive stages of a recipe, thereby avoiding the risk of woody, bitter tastes and optimizing the herb's volatile fragrance. This is a soup that can be cooked with different broths for differing occasions. Chicken broth will give you a hearty soup. Vegetable broth, or mineral water infused with the offcuts and peelings of the leek, carrot, and onion that constitute the soffritto, will give a lighter result.

INGREDIENTS
—*Serves 6*

1 lb. (500g) Puy lentils
2 oz. (50g) diced carrot
2 oz. (50g) diced leek
2 oz. (50g) diced onion
2 oz. (50g) diced heart of celery
Olive oil
Butter
Rosemary
A head of garlic
Bay leaves
2 cups (500ml) broth
2 cups (500ml) lentil water
A mild chili
Fleur de sel, to taste

Wash the lentils thoroughly in a sieve that you can lift in and out of a bowl under a fast-running tap, until the water runs clear. Then cover them in twice their volume of cold water and bring them up to just under a boil. Drain them through a sieve over a sink and refresh the lentils under cold water to halt the cooking. All impurities will thus be purged. Now cover the lentils once more in twice their volume of cold water and bring them up to a simmer. Again drain them, but this time save and reserve the cooking water for the recipe ahead.

For a pound of lentils you will require 4 cups of liquid: 2 cups of chicken broth or vegetable broth, or perhaps mineral water, and another 2 cups made up of the lentil water reserved from the second simmering. Meanwhile, prepare a soffritto. Mandoline a carrot to a thickness equal to that of a lentil, then organize it into julienne and on into a mirepoix. Clean and chop a leek to the same size. Do the same for an onion and a peeled stalk of celery.

Place a copper-bottomed pan over low heat and add a line of olive oil and a knob of butter. Work this around with a branch of freshly picked rosemary to infuse the fats. A crushed clove of garlic or two can feature at this point if you so wish. As can the deseeded flesh of a mild chili. Once the fat starts to bubble and before either the rosemary or garlic even consider coloring or burning, remove them from the pan.

Add the soffritto along with a bay leaf and a new crushed clove of garlic and gently cook to translucent. Add the lentils and raise the heat to medium high. Gently work the ingredients together by moving a flat-edged wooden spoon along the base of the pan. Once the lentils have become one with the soffritto and absorbed the vegetable juices, deglaze the pan with a little of the chosen broth. Allow this to form an emulsion, and then add the remaining broths.

Return to a gentle simmer, until the lentils are cooked al dente. During the season, cloves of young garlic may be added to cook in the simmering soup, or blanched apart and reserved as garnish. Your mind's eye and palate will direct you. One can serve the soup as it is: lentils and finely diced vegetables in a broth, topped with sprigs of bolting parsley and extra virgin olive oil. Or if it is a richer soup you desire, ladle out a quarter of the lentils and vegetables and pass them through a vegetable mill. Return the resultant purée to the pan. And with a whisk to hand, amalgamate the two textures into one hearty soup.

Chicken Broth with Ginger & Chili

When feeling under the weather, this well-seasoned light broth provides a restorative boost. People have raised chickens throughout time without much strain upon their resources. Chickens, given a little space, will transform compost and waste into nutritious eggs and provide flesh and broth for the pot. Chicken broth features in the kitchens of most cultures, and old wives of all creeds champion its curative effect upon the symptoms of the common cold.

I try to start my day with an infusion of boiling mineral water poured upon grated ginger and a spoonful of acacia honey. Ginger and eggs are a great combination. Ginger and chicken broth is almost medicinal. The benefits of ginger make up a list as long as your arm: an anti-inflammatory, immune booster, antioxidant, helps morning sickness, motion sickness, promotes blood circulation, and it is even easy to grow.

In early spring, look out for fresh plump rhizomes of ginger on sale that have little green eyes forming. Soak the rhizome in mineral water overnight to rehydrate, and then cleanly cut it into pieces, with a green-eyed growing bud to each. Plant the ginger root at a hand's depth in a large pot that you can move around and bring in during the winter. It will flower in its second year, so if you desire it as an ornamental resist the temptation to harvest it once the leaves die back. Just bring it in and keep it gently moist. Alternatively, plant lots of ginger and eat as much of it as you can. Freshly harvested ginger is a delicacy to which most are unaccustomed. As you snap a rhizome in your hand it will drop a tear and confirm to the senses that it is immediacy that holds the key to savoring the full potential of an ingredient.

It is the mild flavor of chili that stimulates the palate and is suitable for seasoning. Chili peppers are also easy to grow. They are a self-pollinating fruit that has become an international crop, grown and eaten all over the world. Chilies provide a cheap antibacterial staple packed with high levels of antioxidants, vitamins, and minerals. The fleshier the chili, the milder its flavor will be. To moderate the kick, cut one in half lengthways and remove the seeds and the pith-like membrane. When seasoning, use half or quarter of one, with seeds and pith removed, and lift this out of the broth just as soon as the desired flavor is attained.

INGREDIENTS
—*Serves 6*

4 cups (1l) chicken broth
A knuckle of fresh ginger
A mild chili
Bay leaves
Parsley
Fleur de sel
A dash of extra virgin olive oil

Make a clear chicken broth as described in the introduction to this chapter (page 90). Peel and thinly slice the ginger. Halve the chili lengthways and remove the seeds and pith. Set aside.

Pour the broth into a pan and place over a low flame.

Add the ginger and chili, a bay leaf, and a sprig or two of parsley if so you wish, and gently bring this up to a simmer. Constantly taste the broth as it infuses. Apart from diluting with more liquid, there is no way back from an over-spiced broth.

Once the broth is seasoned to your taste remove the herbs and spices. Serve it directly into heated soup plates; garnish with a fine julienne of the poached ginger and chili, a fresh sprig of parsley, and line of extra virgin olive oil.

Such a broth can obviously be garnished with anything: chicken breast, vegetables, whatever you have to hand.

Rockfish Broth, Saffron & Oysters

This is a broth to enjoy from September until April if you intend oysters as garnish. And you might serve it with a glass of Entre Deux Mers, a white Sauvignon from the region of Bordeaux, which literally translates as "between two seas." Here in southwest France, despite being landlocked, we benefit from local markets that are serviced by fishmongers who have either provisioned themselves at Sète on the Mediterranean or are producers on the Atlantic coast. The French Mediterranean identity is inseparable from the cooking and eating of bouillabaisse, much as French Atlantic identity is closely linked to the consumption of shellfish. This recipe is a celebration of both coasts: Atlantic oysters gently poached in a light Mediterranean fish broth, with an added pinch of saffron to reference the exotic nature of the well-traveled Carcassonne Pass, from Narbonne to the Garonne and on to Bordeaux, which has served as a shortcut and bridge between the two waters for millennia.

Open an oyster, slice through the adductor muscle to release it from the shell, and eat it alive. This is an action that pre-dates cookery and connects us all in a gentle way to our hunting and gathering past. If you jump back a century or two, oysters, just as caviar, were poor man's food. The Thames and the Hudson River were full of natural oyster beds from which any soul brave enough could glean.

An oyster's flavor will vary according to its variety and the quality and salinity of the waters in which it grows. In France, there is a long

tradition of oyster farming. This makes for abundance, variety, and vitality. I am especially keen on pleine mer oysters, which are farmed on high rocks out at sea. These are meaty and crisp in texture with a faint aftertaste of iodine seawater.

It is said that saffron is a mood-enhancing mild hallucinogen. Its euphoric and aphrodisiacal aura may be owed to its exquisite color, like that of the life-giving sun. It has a faintly bitter yet sweet and hay-like flavor. It is the most expensive spice in the world by weight, so beware of being hoodwinked. Avoid powdered saffron and choose traceable stigmas. The stigmas of saffron crocuses are picked by hand, one by one, hence the price. The merest suggestion, that is to say a modest pinch of stigmas, will more than suffice to impart a base note flavor to this broth.

INGREDIENTS
—Serves 6

4 cups (1l) of fish broth
18 oysters
36 stigmas of saffron
A bay leaf
A mild chili
Fleur de sel, to taste

Organize a clear fish broth as described in notes on broth (page 90).

Shuck the oysters over a bowl and retain their juice. Rinse the shucked oysters in their own juice being sure to clean them of errant shell and reserve them for use.

Place the broth in a pan and bring it up to a gentle simmer with a bay leaf and the deseeded flesh of half a chili, tasting as you go.

Be sure to constantly taste the broth as it infuses, for apart from diluting with more liquid there is no way back from an over-spiced broth. Saffron accentuates the taste of salt, so salt sparingly, if at all.

To serve, garnish six pre-heated soup plates with three oysters and half a dozen saffron stigmas each.

Once everybody is assembled and ready, ladle the boiling broth over the oysters and saffron at table. The heat will poach the oysters and color the broth before you.

Pot-au-Feu

There is no limiting season to pot-au-feu. Sometimes one just needs it, restorative gelatinous strength in a bowl. In the introduction to this chapter, I made reference to the timeless action of reaching upon the hearth into an ever-simmering cauldron for a ladle of broth to soak one's bread. When, by way of invitation to table, the Pre–Marshall Plan Gang beckon *"Allons souper!"* from autumn until spring, the meal they serve is from a perpetual stew pot, into which whatever is at hand is cooked.

Luckily, peasant lifestyle enables a homegrown flow of delicacies at hand throughout the year. They raise chickens and fatten a pig, and grow vegetables in soil cared for by generations before them. There is always something. As I write, I am nibbling upon a crust of bread with pâté from the pig we killed together the year before last: two-year-old pâté from an eighteen-month-old beast, fattened on leftovers, potatoes, rocket, and chestnuts. They live virtually self-sufficiently on a diet fit for kings.

So I include pot-au-feu here among soups and broths in celebration of one-pot wonders. You'll need a good cast iron pot with a lid. We'll start it over a low flame and transfer it to the oven, shamelessly breaking rules as we go.

Oxtail or veal tail is a cut of meat very rich in gelatin. It requires gentle simmering and makes an excellent base for soup.

Bone marrow is life-giving, flexible tissue. It generates blood cells and is a key component of the lymphatic system, which regulates the metabolism and supports the body's immune system. An old staple of healthy cooking is marrowbone broth. However be warned: cook this somewhere you are happy to have the pronounced aroma colonize, for it requires a day or three of gentle simmering. A slug of vinegar in the water helps draw calcium and minerals from the bones, and freshens the air. A keen and watchful eye must be kept to the adding of water little by little when and as needed. Finally, once you have endowed your kitchen, your house, and even perhaps your street with the odor of boiled bones, strain the broth through muslin. Once cold it will set, and you will be able to lift the fat from the surface. Reserve this potent brew and use it as a medicinal base broth for any soup you choose.

For a side dish to pot-au-feu, roast some extra hind-shank marrowbones cut into lengths of a couple of inches each. You'll need to dust the bones in a little flour seasoned with grated Javanese pepper and finely chopped sage. Then in an iron-handled pan, seize, and color them top and tail in oil and butter infused with bay. Transfer the pan down to a hot oven for twenty minutes or so until the marrow releases from the bone and is gelatinous in texture. Serve on grilled bread seasoned with fleur de sel and parsley flowers. Shank of veal is a flavorsome, nutritious, gelatinous, and inexpensive cut that requires long, slow cooking. The shank is cut from the upper portion of the leg. The fore shank has a thinner bone and thereby carries a higher proportion of meat. As a rule I use fore shank for the pot-au-feu, and roast the bones of the hind shank, which are wider and carry more marrow, for finger food garnish.

Have your butcher saw the fore shank into slices of a generous thickness, and saw slices twice as thick again from the hind shank for marrowbone.

Although not truly a pot-au-feu or a dish of braised veal, this recipe tips its hat at both and more than holds its own against either.

INGREDIENTS
—Serves 6

2 stalks of lemongrass
2 knuckles of ginger
Bay leaves
2 mild chilis
An oxtail, or preferably a veal tail
A fore-shank of veal sliced on the marrowbone
Vegetables to compose a soffritto (see page 90)
Extra virgin olive oil
Butter
Mineral water, or marrowbone broth
An onion
A generous bunch of parsley
A hindshank cut in lengths of at least two inches thick for a roasted bone marrow finger food side dish
Sourdough bread to toast

Firstly organize a mirepoix for your soffritto. Onion, carrot, and leek will do. You can add celery to this if you wish but be aware that it will impart its pronounced taste. I replace it with finely diced parsley stalks, whose flavor I prefer. Cut the lemongrass in half lengthways, and bruise it with the back of a knife. Organize a knuckle of ginger, a branch of fresh bay leaves, and remove the seeds and pith from a mild chili.

Inspect the meat and where necessary trim the tail and shank of dried fat and blemishes. When you have all the above ingredients before you, commence.

Place the cocotte over a moderate heat and add olive oil and butter. As they melt, infuse these fats with bay, chili, ginger, and lemongrass. Remove the herbs and proceed to brown the meats on all sides, in batches if necessary, with an eye to temperature so as no burning may occur.

Remove the meats with a slotted spoon; add the soffritto to the cocotte and once again the herbs. Gently cook to translucent, and then neatly garnish the cocotte with the browned meats. Add mineral water, or marrowbone broth, to barely cover the contents and bring the resulting liquid up to a gentle simmer. Skim off any impurities that rise to the surface with a ladle. Retrieve the herbs and spices and replace them with fresh ones.

Maroon these upon an island formed out of a halved onion, the root of your leek, and a generous bunch of parsley perched atop the meats and liquid. In this way their taste will not be condensed in the broth, but rather their flavor will inform the steam that circulates under the closed lid throughout the period of long slow cooking. You might change the herbs each time you cast an eye on progress.

Close the cocotte with its lid and place it in a low oven at 300°F (150°C) for a good couple of hours. You know it's done when the meat melts away from the bone.

If you desire a thicker sauce, remove the meats and reduce the broth. In such an instance an olive oil and mineral water mashed potato (pages 206–207) makes a fine accompaniment, or, if you are feeling Milanese, conjure a saffron risotto (cooked with the broth, and mantecato with bone marrow).

My preference is to simply bring the cocotte to table with a ladle, garnished with a scattering of finely chopped parsley and a dusting of mild chili, and serve it as a broth. Accompanied by a dish of roast bone marrow on toast for all to share.

Chilled Melon & Cardamom

Melon season bridges June, July, and August. Melons are thirsty sun-bathers rich in potassium and vitamins A and C. Growing them on any kind of scale is risky business. One freak hailstorm and a perfect patch will be annihilated as if by machine-gun fire. They demand attention and care. As with much relating to fruit and orchards, success with melons calls for a fair wind and an arm extend to Lady Luck.

The European cantaloupe, *Cucumis melo cantalupensis*, was developed in the Vatican gardens for the papal table during the eighteenth century. For this soup, I use yellow *Charentais* melon, which is a French variety derived from the cantaloupe. Many of my neighbors grow this prized variety as a commercial crop. This is hard work, which involves a rhythm of harvesting ripening melons in the cool of dawn, all summer long, to maintain supply to local markets.

A defining quality of melons—and the same applies to peaches—is that they hold no starch, which means that once they are harvested they ripen no further. The maturation into a perfectly ripe fruit needs to happen whilst still attached to the mother vine. It is the last day or two that is vital. So think twice before wasting hard-earned money at a supermarket fruit counter. A melon picked green is never going to generate the necessary sugars to ripen and produce the incomparable sweetness that is a perfectly ripe melon. There is no hint of bitter after-taste or any trace of acidity; ripe fruit seduces the eye, then the nose, and tastes just as it smells.

Cardamom, native to southwest India, is an herbaceous perennial plant that grows no permanent stem or trunk above ground and composts back to soil level once it has flowered. It is the seedpod of the plant that is harvested. These seedpods mature at staggered intervals and must be picked by hand. Consequently, like saffron and vanilla, cardamom is expensive. Luckily, the faintest suggestion goes a long way. If and when you find quality spices, in general it is a good idea to stock up. A hint of the best will always be more than enough. Cardamom and melon are a heaven-sent couple; a twist of Javanese pepper completes the trinity.

Javanese pepper, or long pepper, was used as a spice in the West before the subsequent import of now familiar peppercorns—it has a more refined if somewhat hotter flavor. They are about half an inch long and rather slim, resembling a catkin, the young flower of the hazelnut tree. They should be kept airtight in a jar, and grated freshly when used. Their effect upon the flavor of fruit, especially strawberry and melon, is enhancing.

INGREDIENTS
—*Serves 6*

3 Charentais melons
6 cardamom pods, crushed and bound in muslin
The seeds of 2 cardamom pods finely ground for seasoning
A Javanese long pepper
Fleur de sel, to taste

Bring a large pan of water, salted to two tablespoons per quart (thirty-five grams per liter), to a boil. Into this add the crushed seeds of six cardamom pods wrapped in a muslin pouch.

Open a ripe melon and deseed it with a spoon. Place these flavorsome seeds in a square patch of muslin, tie it up neatly into a bundle with string, and add to the boiling water. They will flavor the cooking liquid.

With a sharp filleting knife detail the melons into quarters and then eighths. Blanch these for barely a minute in the boiling water. Do this in batches if the quantity is such that it would take the water below a boil.

Place a vegetable mill over a bain-marie sitting in a bowl of ice. Lift the melon out of the cauldron with a spider, and pass it immediately through the vegetable mill so the pulp and juice fall directly into the iced bain-marie.

This must all be done quickly. The melon will have had its color seized by the salt, and been subtly perfumed with cardamom. Cover and stand to chill.

Separately, remove the seeds from two additional pods of cardamom and grind finely in a mortar and pestle. Prior to serving, adjust the seasoning of the soup with ground cardamom, Javanese pepper, and fleur de sel. This is a soup for a high summer lunch.

SAVORY FIRST COURSES

———— ✦ ————

WHITE & BROWN CRAB SALAD

✳

CAESAR SALAD

✳

GREEN WALNUTS WITH CHICORY, APPLE & ROQUEFORT

✳

STEAMED YOUNG LEEKS, ALLIUM FLOWER VINAIGRETTE

✳

WILD SEA TROUT, WATERCRESS & HORSERADISH

✳

TUNA TARTARE, CUCUMBER & WHITE PEACH

✳

KNIFE-CUT STEAK TARTARE

✳

UNDRESSED FIGS, PAPER-THIN PROSCUITTO,
PARSLEY & BORAGE

✳

BALTIC HERRING, APPLE & CRÈME FRAÎCHE

First Courses

A first course is a somewhat ritualistic and formal affair, but it can be fun. It all depends on who is sitting next to you. We are conditioned to consider multiple courses the norm in restaurants and at dinner parties. But service à la russe, food served in a sequence of courses, was only adopted in the West in the nineteenth century. Previously, a multitude of dishes would arrive at once, in one big splurge. Everybody politely drew their blades and tucked in.

A first course breaks a meal down into three acts. It gives occasion to serve different wines and draws the ritual of dinner out into an elegant and civilized affair, with time for conversation with those seated on either side of you. In a domestic context this is largely omitted, as is the act of coming to table at all.

A savory first course is a practical way to cater for large numbers. It is something that you can prepare in advance which frees you up to focus on the main course while your guests distract one another with small talk, knock back cocktails, and guzzle finger food.

Compose your menu according to the occasion. For social gatherings with networking and preening, a first course of five bites will suffice. For a harvest feast where hospitality is measured in one-upmanship of generosity, judge accordingly.

Whatever the occasion and regardless of the quantity, the objective of a first course is to open the appetite and stimulate digestion for the main course and dessert to follow. It is an opportunity to mark a time, a place, and a mood by serving clean and textured flavors.

White & Brown Crab Salad

Every last morsel of a crab, apart from the gills, can be put to culinary use. Crabs are omnivores. Their diet consists primarily of algae, mollusks, and crustaceans supplemented by scavenging. Octopus and man are their only real foes.

The way to differentiate between males and females is to cast an eye at their abdomen. In males this is narrow and triangular in form, whereas the females are broader and rounded; this allows them to brood fertilized eggs. Females do their nails and have bright red tips to their claws; males do not. Hen crabs (females) are typically rich in brown meat; cock crabs (males), with their larger claws, yield more white meat. The brown meat (stored in the head shell) is where the taste is to be found, the white meat is the source of succulence, texture, and flavor.

Crabs are caught year-round, yet eating crab suggests itself to me more in autumn and early winter, before their breeding season starts and vitality is given over to roe. Once they have mated, the females brood their eggs for the eight months it takes them to hatch. Those who manage to avoid net and pot typically live for twenty-five years or more, and some much longer. There are tales of crabs living to be a hundred.

When you purchase live crab, the best and kindest way to store them is under a cold, damp dishcloth scattered with ice in a crate on a cool floor. If you are squeamish about plunging live crabs into boiling water, first dispatch them by inserting the tip of a knife between their eyes and twisting. Which is hardly less gruesome. Cooks hold a rather one-sided godly power in this situation; so let it fall upon you and your conscience to decide.

As we have seen in the recipe for *plateau de fruits de mer*, protein is delicate and diminished by prolonged exposure to high temperatures. So, when poaching crabs and lobsters pay close attention to temperature. To boil them is to purge them of their succulence; to poach is to poach, not to boil.

INGREDIENTS
—*Serves 4*

A cock crab
A hen crab
A head of Florence fennel
Ingredients for mayonnaise (page 82)
Fines herbes to garnish

To cook crab, bring to a boil a large pot of water, salted to two tablespoons per quart (thirty-five grams per liter).

Gently place the crabs into rolling boiling water, feet first. If a crab enters the water on its back, its head is liable to become waterlogged in the pot, which compromises the dark meat in the head shell. Whether this is true or a tall tale and merely matter of ritual is up for debate. What is for certain, though, is that ritual, detail, and method are all assets in the kitchen. They bring a backbeat of structure to the act of cooking, a trained reflex that becomes rhythmic with repetition, freeing up the mind to the imagination. Adding the cold crab to the boiling water will cause an immediate drop in water temperature. Turn off the heat and cover the pot with a lid, standing to gently poach for ten minutes to the pound (twenty to the kilogram).

The moment the pincer will pull from the claw free of meat, the crab is cooked. Remove the crab from the pot and stand it to strain in a colander. It is easier to clean crabs whilst they are still warm, before the meat sets to the shell. Systematically separate the crabs into three bowls: legs, claws, and heads. Pick the white meat from the claws and the legs. Cover and reserve.

Lift the head shell away from the skull and scoop out the brown meat with a small spoon. With a pair of good scissors remove the lungs (the dead ladies' fingers running along either side of the skull). Pick the skull for white meat. Any meat that you miss is not wasted, as it will flavor a broth. Check the brown meat for errant cartilage, shell, and general unsavory scrap. Chop finely and set it aside.

To make a broth, which might be used to upgrade any leftovers the following day, or as a dainty accompaniment to your salad, cover the picked skulls with mineral water and bring them to a very gentle simmer, skimming the surface until it runs clear. Never boil. As for most broths, the ideal ratio of liquid to matter is equal parts one to one. Simmer until the desired flavor is attained, then take off the heat and stand to rest. This broth makes a wonderful first course garnished with white meat, an herb or two, a pinch of salt, and a line of olive oil.

Using a mandoline, shave Florence fennel vertically from root to fan, into harp shapes, thickly enough to yield good crunch. Refresh these in iced water awhile to crisp.

Make a mayonnaise (page 82), incorporating some of the dark meat, and perhaps stretching the emulsion to desired consistency with a splash of broth. Garnish with chopped chervil and parsley and a fine dice of any leftover Florence fennel. Assemble your salad and serve.

Caesar Salad

Caesar salad is a menu classic. You see it on room service menus, in airport bars, in restaurants, on television, although not often at the kitchen table. Caesar salad has become a universal idea; it has morphed into a general concept, with the emphasis on general. It is rarely the ephemeral and textured umami salad that it can be.

The name jumps at the eye. There is a familiarity to it, which alleviates the panic and distraction of being passed a menu. "Are you ready to order sir?" "Well, no, I haven't even looked yet . . . Um, OK, the Caesar salad!" Ordered not in desire and anticipation, but in hope. A Caesar salad is an exercise in assemblage, which is the very reason it often fails in restaurants. The quality of its component parts is vital. An assemblage of generic produce will taste of just that.

To make one properly you'll need a romaine lettuce with a big heart. They are available year-round. If you are growing them in a garden, the season will be from late spring to mid-summer. The romaine has two textures: the base of the leaf is ribbed and crisp, the higher part is green leaf. A prize romaine yields a milky, mildly bitter, savory liquid, rising from its root stem to the ribs of its outer leaves.

Parmesan, or Parmigiano-Reggiano, is a hard cheese made from raw cow's milk matured anywhere from twelve to thirty-six months. Like Champagne, the name Parmesan is connected to a geographic region, copyrighted, and jealously guarded with protected designation of origin status (PDO). The best Parmesan is made from the best milk and the best milk is obtained from animals grazing natural pasture.

Anchovies packed in salt offer the best eating and are preferable over those sold in oil or brine, where rancidity often lurks. Anchovies assigned for salting are prize specimens; gutted and air-dried to purge excess liquid, then packed in salt.

There is one particularly fine brand of anchovy paste, made from salted anchovies ground to a paste in a mortar and pestle. One can do it oneself, yet since 1850, when a gentleman named Cesare Balena in Florence, Italy, commercialized his namesake recipe, there has been no need.

INGREDIENTS
—*Serves 4*

A head of romaine lettuce
2 salted anchovies, washed and filleted
Parmesan, grated and shaved
Fines herbes for garnish
An egg yolk
A spike of Dijon mustard
Anchovy paste
Extra virgin olive oil

Once you are back from the garden, lettuce in hand, and have washed it in cold water and liberated it from slugs and wildlife, halve it by making an incision an inch from the base. In one controlled action, delicately pull the lettuce apart. It will rip as it comes, which will give the leaves of the finished salad a natural line that pleases the eye. Repeat the gesture into quarters and eighths.

To prepare the salted anchovy fillets—they are whole and still wearing their heads—rinse them thoroughly under cold water. Then lift the fillets off the bone; they will surrender easily.

The dressing for Caesar salad is essentially a stretched mayonnaise, flavored with anchovy and grated Parmesan. If you leave the lettuce a little wet after washing, I find this to have a sufficient lengthening effect upon the mayonnaise.

If you so wish, lengthen the mayonnaise with half a ladle of chicken, lobster, or crab broth. This can be spiced to taste and serve as a means to qualify the base taste of your salad. This is relevant only when composing a garnished Caesar salad: of chicken, or lobster, or any other such distracting additions. To my palette it is enough to stick with the trinity of lettuce, Parmesan, and anchovy.

Croutons are to be forgotten. They are waiter props that feign texture to limp lettuce. If someone insists on croutons: cut the crusts off a loaf; if it is a couple of days stale all the better as it will hold form and be easier to cut. Detail an equal-sized dice of bread and add these to a blistering hot, cast-iron pan. Shake the pan in a back and forth action constantly; the bread must dance. As it crisps—this will happen quickly—add seasoning: a little salt and the faintest hint of olive oil.

Bring an egg yolk, olive oil, and mustard to room temperature for the mayonnaise. Organize before you all the elements of your salad. Finely grate some Parmesan cheese, and use a vegetable peeler to conjure a bowl of Parmesan shavings. Julienne and dice the salted anchovy fillets.

Combine the yolk and mustard in a bowl, add a squeeze of Balena and then commence to pour in the olive oil, and whisk. In a gentle and deliberate manner, form an emulsion of oil and yolk, with a sharp eye to consistency, all whilst whisking your dressing to life.

You might add grated Parmesan, which will tighten the consistency. You can counteract this by adding a little mineral water or just by shaking your lettuce at it. Continue in this vein until you deem the quantity of your dressing to be sufficient to the volume of lettuce.

Correct the seasoning with grated Parmesan, diced anchovy, even Balena. Taste as you go and season to your palate, which will evolve with season and mood and age and context. The same dish seasoned for your children, your boss, and then for yourself and eaten alone, will likely find quite distinct expression each time.

Add the lettuce to the mayonnaise and toss to combine. Adjust the consistency of the dressing as necessary with a little mineral water or grated cheese. Add the Parmesan shavings, the julienned fillets of anchovy, parsley, and flowering chives. Now eat it while it's crisp and cold, as salad should be.

Green Walnuts with Chicory, Apple & Roquefort

Walnut season starts, depending on the year, and give or take a week or two, around about mid-September. As with all nuts, when they are freshly harvested, texture and flavor are optimal, as they are fully hydrated with the sap of the mother tree. To improve dried nuts, stand them to steep awhile either in mineral water or live milk.

Roquefort is a blue cheese made from ewe's milk. Just as with Parmesan in the previous recipe, Roquefort is also a geographical place, high in the Massif Central of France, and the cheese made there is made to exacting specifications and benefits from PDO status.

Legend has it that the passing of a beautiful girl entranced a shepherd boy from Roquefort, causing him to abandon his picnic in the cave where he was sheltering. When he returned several months later, now a man, the plain cheese he had left behind had turned blue. *Penicillium roqueforti*, bacteria present in the soil of the caves, had spun its magic.

Later, cheese makers would leave bread in the caves until it became thoroughly covered with mold. This mold was then subtly introduced into the cheese-making process. Left to mature, it gives the cheese its distinctive coloring and fine salty, sweet, mild tang.

Apple and Roquefort thrown together with a faintly bitter endive quenches the palate with its crisp watery texture and, tossed in walnut oil and lemon juice, makes a super simple salad that tastes like a million dollars.

INGREDIENTS
—Serves 4

2 endive
2 tart apples
12 new-season walnuts
Roquefort cheese, to taste
A dash of walnut oil
The juice of half a lemon
Fleur de sel

Shell and halve the walnuts. With a sharp knife halve the endives along the vertical, and again around the waist. Roughly chop the coarser lower parts and finely chop the delicate tops.

Crumble Roquefort between your fingers as it comes. Peel, core, halve, quarter, and eighth the apples.

Whisk together walnut oil and lemon juice with a pinch of salt to form your dressing. Combine and serve.

The key to this salad is walnut season. In walnut season this is a salad that will have your taste buds hitting every note on the scale, leaving them ravished in its wake. Save it for autumn.

Steamed Young Leeks, Allium Flower Vinaigrette

This is a timeless bistro classic of *la vielle France*. The sort of springtime savory first course that would be served executed to perfection at a roadside petrol station in the days before highways and multinational chains. The days when a gas station might be an independently owned family business with a vegetable garden out back. Grandma behind the stove, serving the day's menu from high noon until it ran out. Places that to be found nowadays, incur driving deep into the sticks to worlds sheltered and autonomous.

Poireaux au vinaigrette, young spring leeks thinned from a row to surrender room and light to sturdier brethren, make for fine April eating. You will find new-season baby leeks for sale in abundance at farmers' markets at this time of year. Their timing is impeccable as it coincides with the bolting and flowering of their allium cousins, the chive. Perhaps you have leeks left over from the winter in your own garden; they will have by now bolted and sent up high, great bulbous flowered fists of seed.

INGREDIENTS
—Serves 4

16 young leeks
A clove of garlic
An onion
A bunch of chives
Chive, onion, garlic, or leek flowers, if you can find them
Fleur de sel
Extra virgin olive oil
A spike of Dijon mustard
A dash of rice vinegar

Spring leeks, steamed, or perhaps better briskly blanched in abundant boiling water salted to two tablespoons per quart (thirty-five grams per liter). And once cooked, halved along the length, to garnish a snugly fitting serving dish.

Concoct a lively vinaigrette to your taste; garlic is another allium cousin, as is onion. On a clean and orderly chopping board, organize before you a very fine dice of onion, chives, and a squeezed clove of garlic. In a large mixing bowl, with a whisk to hand, emulsify energetically extra virgin olive oil, an invisible spike of Dijon mustard, and rice vinegar. Incorporate the squeezed garlic, dice of onion, and chive. Pour this upon the leeks whilst still warm.

If you take a halved leek in one hand and a fork in the other, you might in one gesture slide a fork along the length of the leek and thus detail it into long thin tender strands, leaving them conjoined at the root head. This allows the dressing to penetrate and season the leeks throughout and pleases the eye as a curiosity: leeks morphed into nests of tentacles. Garnish with allium flowers and serve.

Wild Sea Trout, Watercress & Horseradish

Sea trout and brown trout are the same species, *Salmo trutta*. What determines whether or not they migrate out to sea remains a mystery. I have always imagined the moment of decision in the mind of a young trout, of those who have the balls (sea trout are predominantly female), the spirit of adventure and daring that it takes to leave a stream for a river, to adapt to salt water, to swim out on the tide of an estuary, and make life at sea. Perhaps an instinctive pursuit for a richer diet of shrimp and crustaceans is worth risking fin and gill, only to return to the fresh waters of the natal stream a year later to spawn. Unlike salmon, though, sea trout do not die after spawning. They return to the sea each year, returning home a few pounds heavier to spawn again. Such is the cycle of their adult lives.

They are caught from April onwards to early autumn. My father's birthday fell on 17 July. In Wales, this is sea trout season, haymaking time, the garden a carpet of wild strawberries. Madeira birthday cake built high into a leaning tower of peppered wild strawberries and minted whipped cream.

This was also a time of year when the watercress bed was in full production. It was planted by my mother a short walk downstream through Col-brook, the dingle below the farm. A few yards of cool shallow water, fed by its own spring. The cress quickly took root and thrived. Watercress is heralded as a cure-all: an antiviral tonic, an antioxidant, a diuretic, and a stimulant packed with vitamins and minerals. Hippocrates, the father of western medicine, heralded watercress for its healing properties as the "cure of all cures." His first hospital reputedly built beside a spring so to grow watercress to feed his patients.

Adjacent to our watercress bed was a bank of horseradish, irreversibly established years earlier. Horseradish, like its Asian cousin wasabi, likes water and well-drained sandy soil. The leaves grow quickly to waist height, sending up delicate white flowers before dying back in autumn. The flowers make a tisane that wards off the common cold. Through winter the plant consolidates its forces in the sugars and starches gained through leaf and photosynthesis, and holds them in the root. The rhizomes spread quickly in an invasive manner. Planted somewhere appropriate, this is a dream that makes for plenty. The older roots send out runners that send up new plants. These tender youngsters make the best eating, grated and used instantly. The volatile spicy flavor is lost to the air. So make your sauce swiftly.

INGREDIENTS
—*Serves 4*

A side of wild sea trout deboned and trimmed; slivered to the gauge and texture you desire
A bunch of watercress washed and stood to drain

HORSERADISH SAUCE:
A root of horseradish, peeled and finely grated
Crème frâiche
Horseradish flavored rice vinegar
Dijon mustard

Finely grate the horseradish root and leave it to macerate in very little rice vinegar spiked with a hint of Dijon mustard, incorporate the very minimum of crème fraîche, and that's it: an anti-inflammatory, antioxidant, full of vitamins and minerals that stimulates digestion.

Sea trout, filleted and sliced paper-thin, eaten raw and served with a bunch of peppery watercress and a horseradish sauce. These three streamside ingredients make for a delectable combination. A clean-flavored, palette-stimulating first course for an outside summer dinner, an invigorating picnic served to the middle of the family table, even a clandestine snack. Accompanied by a well-shod ice bucket of mineral, dry, crisp textured white wine.

Tuna Tartare, Cucumber & White Peach

If you spot a tuna at the fish market, keep your eye peeled for the muscle behind its head. It is a prized and tender morsel. That of a bonito is an equally good catch. The Japanese revere this muscle; western white man is largely without reference to it, aspiring rather to the lean and comparably flavorless loin. And make sure the fish is fresh; this is not a dish for Mondays. You won't catch a cat eating a stale mouse.

INGREDIENTS
—*Serves 4*

½ lb. (225g) tuna
A white peach
Half a cucumber, deseeded and peeled
A lime, filleted and diced
Tender shoots of young parsley
Chive and parsley flowers

KOSHO DRESSING:
A dash of soy sauce
A dash of extra virgin olive oil
Grated ginger to taste
A spike of kosho paste
The juice of a freshly squeezed lime, to taste
A fine dice of sweet onion, for body

Cut the tuna into equal-sized squares with a razor-sharp knife. Employ one controlled action, allowing the blade to perform its role. No pressure is required, merely direction. Let the knife do the work. Heavy-handed chopping has no merit. The ingredient's cell walls, if crushed, bruised, and bleeding, will no longer hold shape. This translates to loss of texture, rapid aging, and diminished allure. Maintain a razor-sharp filleting knife amongst your tools for all delicate chopping. Knives are as extensions to the hands.

To fillet the lime, first undress it by squaring it head and tail, to cut away the zest and pith. Then take the naked lime in one hand and a filleting knife in the other. Insert the knife along the inner wall of the membrane that holds the fillets together, and proceed to lift them free, one by one. Cut the summer peach and cucumber to an equal-sized dice; they bring crisp texture and a certain sweet acidity to a tuna tartare. Assemble and season the tartare in a big mixing bowl just prior to serving, combining the ingredients with gentle hand and economy of gesture. Dress with parsley flowers, chive flowers, and lime.

You might concoct a dressing with soy, olive oil, diced sweet onion, grated ginger, lime juice, kosho paste (fermented minced rind of salted yuzu and chili). The proportions of oil to soy to kosho and lime are best geared to your mood and palate. The objective is to underscore and enhance the main ingredients, not drown them out. So whisk together a loose emulsion; all whilst keeping it subtle and clean.

This delicate dish makes a great first course for a summer lunch. Serve generous spoonfuls of tartare upon chilled plates at the very last minute—once guests are already seated at table. Choose a pretty jug for the dressing, so guests may help themselves.

Knife-Cut Steak Tartare

Steak tartare is all about the texture and flavor of its component parts. A razor-sharp knife will extend the hand to the eye's design. And then there is the quality of the meat. Cows are herbivores. The ideal is to select beef that has been fattened on a natural diet. Beef or pink veal, which is to say veal that has been milk fed under the mother for the first six months of its life and then turned out to pasture. This change in the diet to grass blushes the color of the animal's meat, from milk white on across a palette ever pinker, to red.

Meat from hormone- and antibiotic-pumped retired dairy feedlot animals that have spent their short lives standing on concrete ankle-deep in their own shit eating corn- and soya-based feed and silage—fermented grass, which gives them livers like those of alcoholics—does not appeal to the senses. Do not eat this at all, let alone raw.

Choose a tender cut: the pear, the spider, a butcher's cut, if you are in time that is, and your butcher likes you. Otherwise some other early bird will surely have passed before you and been given first dibs. Alternatively you might use rump, but choose something flavorsome; avoid fillet. I will always ask a new butcher what he recommends. If his eyes twinkle and he presents you with a fillet of beef, his girth and greed have skipped a step ahead of his palate and integrity.

INGREDIENTS
—*Serves 4*

ALL CUT TO AN EVEN SIZED DICE AND DOSED TO TASTE
1 lb. (450g) of tender flavorsome grass fed beef
An egg yolk
Dijon mustard
Sweet onion
Capers
Gherkins
Parsley
Worcestershire sauce
Tabasco
Chili
Extra virgin olive oil
Fleur de sel

The classic seasoning of a beef tartare runs as follows. The yolk of an egg, strong Dijon mustard, sweet salad onion, capers, and gherkins, all diced with precision for texture. Finely chopped parsley and a little Worcestershire sauce may be added for umami, as is often a splash of Tabasco for spice. A fine dusting of the deseeded flesh of a chili achieves the latter rather better.

Detail the meat first into lengths and then cut them horizontally into a generously proportioned dice of equal size. It is worth spending the time to do this properly; a knife-cut tartare leaves mincing pretenders in the shade.

Start with a yolk in a mixing bowl; add the faintest splash of extra virgin olive oil, followed by the finely diced seasonings. Check this for salt, and then add the meat. Correct the seasoning to your taste: umami Worcestershire sauce, Tabasco if you must (if so, preferably the green). More mustard, taste again and that's it.

In a restaurant, steak tartare is served with either pommes frites or a salade verte. An herb flower salad is my preference, with extra mustard for the table, and slices of ephemeral toast. One plate to share is often enough; this is a raw and highly seasoned dish to taste and share rather than to gorge upon.

Undressed Figs, Paper-Thin Prosciutto, Parsley & Borage

What most Italian guidebooks do not tell you is that in vernacular dialect, *la fica*, (from the Latin *Ficus carica*) is to be found not on a tree, but rather between a woman's legs. The adoption of this vernacular in antiquity had, for reasons of propriety, the extraordinary effect of creating an exception to one of the rules of Italian syntax: that a tree is male and the fruit it bears is female. So if you find yourself in polite circles at a summer table, when passing the fruit to the left, think to offer your neighbor *un fico* and not *una fica*. Forewarned is forearmed.

Come late summer, figs suddenly ripen all at once in an almighty glut. They are, by far, best eaten straight from the tree, grazing, for breakfast perhaps, or dessert on the hoof. Dried figs, fig jam, and other such nutritious larder fare are the focus of much commercial production, and invariably taste overwhelmingly sweet.

At Tibas there are fig trees in the orchard, both green and black that bear fruit during four to six weeks each year. The black variety are smaller, their texture more condensed, their flavor richer. The green are refined, though a combination of the two is what I usually serve, as it is what I have got.

A fruit hook—a cast iron claw mounted upon a cane—serves to extend the arm's reach. These exist in an array of shapes, sizes, and lengths. They are hand-forged and bespoke to the shape or variety of tree and the gauge of its branches. Allowing a perfect specimen to be prized from upon high, and out of the path of circling hornets, all in one smooth gesture. Hornets adore figs. Seemingly overnight they will colonize a sheltered nearby spot, and build great basketball-shaped paper nests to commute from. When figs are left unpicked—to over-ripen and ferment—great marauding swarms of drunken hornets ensue. Once stung, twice shy! Be vigilant, one sting is agony, a dozen fatal.

When they are in season and bought locally, figs are plentiful and cheap. They are also a ready source of fiber, calcium, vitamins, and minerals, but they neither keep nor travel, so embrace the moment. The tree originated in Asia and extends fragrant elephant-eared modesty-yielding leaves. It will grow rapidly pretty much anywhere, the sunnier the better.

Borage thrives like a weed in a kitchen garden, self-seeds, and multiplies freely. Bees love it; traditionally borage is planted near hives to improve yields. Both the leaves and the flowers are edible. They make good grazing and lend themselves well to herb salads and cocktails. They have a mild flavor of iodine, invoking cucumber, not dissimilar to the aftertaste of a good oyster. Borage has a demulcent soothing quality. Recognized as a restorative to purge melancholy, it is deemed to revive and cheer the heart.

Prosciutto is salt-cured pork that can be made with a multitude of cuts. The classic is made with the hind leg, the ham. Culatello is made from a chosen cut of buttock or rump; guanciale is made with the cheeks, capocollo with the rolled neck fillet, and so on. What counts is the quality of the pork and that of the salt and skill of the hand used in the seasoning. Salting is a master's art (think caviar). Bargains are to be had at fancy delicatessens selling top quality prosciutto. The end of a ham near the hock, where all the ligaments come down to join the knee knuckle, these pack flavor and make the best eating. Yet they will not yield great, big, lean and elegant slices and as a result are often to be found for sale, as bin ends. Fist-sized treasures, sold for a fraction of the price. Again keep sharp eyes firmly fixed to the counter.

A prosciutto knife with its nimbly balanced center of gravity, for obvious reasons makes for rapid progress. A meat slicer set to number one renders greater satisfaction still. A sliver or a slice cut from the very same ham offers sensorial experiences quite distinct. Cut thickly, so as to chew on, the fat and flesh of salt-cured pork is an umami affair. Rustic picnic fodder perhaps: a crust of bread, a hock of prosciutto, a snifter of wine. Sliced paper-thin, to the texture of gold leaf, prosciutto is transformed, ephemeral seasoned shawls to enrobe succulent figs.

So, with the best tool you have to hand, and, as close to the hour of eating as possible, organize an abundance of prosciutto sliced as thinly as you can.

INGREDIENTS
—*Serves 4*

Prosciutto, sliced paper-thin
6 figs, sliced to a generous sashimi-size gauge
Basil, parsley, or arugula leaves
Borage flowers
Extra virgin olive oil
Fleur de sel

Figs and prosciutto is a classic and unimpeachable combination. To execute the dish, focus on texture. Paper-thin prosciutto, generous sashimi-gauged slices of fig, parsley to clean the palate, a leaf or two of basil as mild spice, and borage to lift the heart.

Baltic Herring, Apple & Crème Fraîche

The Baltic Sea was once famous for the size and quality of its herring. The name remains iconic, though the sea now struggles with industrial pollution and alarming levels of dioxins. Most commercial herring are currently fished out of the Northern Atlantic and Pacific Oceans. In these clean waters, herring exist in great shoals. The late great gluttonous Otto von Bismarck said: "If herring were as expensive as caviar, the whole wide world would celebrate its taste." A larder without herring is bare.

They can be eaten salted, soused, pickled, or smoked. As such they have been a staple, transportable fish through time. Herring is a supremely adaptable fish. Freshly caught, herring is good filleted and cut into strips, breaded, deep-fried, and served with a squeeze of lime or tartar sauce.

The French classic *hareng pomme à l'huile*, is a dish of lightly smoked herring served with warm boiled potatoes and raw onion, seasoned with olive oil and vinegar—wine or champagne—and left to macerate awhile. Served with chives. *Kipper* refers to the process, not the fish. To kipper is to salt, to spice, to air dry, or to smoke, thus what can be kippered is limited only by the imagination. Cold-smoked kippered herring is a delicacy. Warmed in a low oven and brushed with good butter.

Rollmop herring is my choice. They are neither expensive nor hard to find. You can concoct them yourself, though this is best left to those with a ready supply of fresh fish. The optimum window is the summer months of May, June, and July, prior to breeding season, before the fish's vitality is given over to its roe. Take care to source them unsweetened, free of barnacled sugar. A butterflied herring wrapped around onion and gherkin closed with a peg. Choice rollmops are pickled tart, with good vinegar, salt, onion, peppercorns, mustard seeds, and bay. It is enough to reach for a jar, twist open a lid, and, armed with an apple and a spoon of cream, to rustle up a delectable feast at any hour of the day, all in a matter of minutes. It is as easy to make for two as for twelve.

INGREDIENTS
—Serves 4

4 butterflied rollmop herrings
Pickled onion, from the marinade
2 tart apples, peeled, cored, and finely sliced
Crème fraîche
Parsley
Milled black pepper

Rollmops are traditionally served with a crisp, thinly sliced apple and crème-fraîche. Seasoned with ground black pepper, the finely diced pickled onions from the marinade, parsley, and that's it. This is an old-school brasserie dish, still found on menus as Baltic, Bismarck, or Matjes Herring. It can be a strategic thing to order in a restaurant, one that you may go to for the atmosphere as much as the food. This is a dish that requires no cooking, and as such cannot be screwed up. The grand Parisian and Viennese European institutions that remain offer a spectacle of professional waiter service to behold. If you order oysters, *hareng baltique*, and a bottle of Sancerre, not much can go wrong. Sit at a banquette and take it all in.

RISOTTI E SPAGHETTI

RISOTTO ALLA PARMIGIANA

*

RISOTTO ALLO ZAFFERANO

*

RISOTTO OSTRICHE E PREZZEMOLO

*

RISOTTO AL GRANCHIO

*

RISOTTO POMODORO, MOZZARELLA DI BUFALA,
FIORI DI BASILICO

SPAGHETTI ALLE VONGOLE

*

SPAGHETTI AL POMODORO

*

SPAGHETTI ALLA CARBONARA

*

SPAGHETTI CON BOTTARGA

*

SPAGHETTI AGLIO, OLIO E PEPERONCINO

Cooking Risotto

Risotto is a dish of rice cooked in broth. As the rice cooks, it releases starch. When fat is added to this starch, in the form of olive oil, butter, or a base, it forms a flavor-carrying emulsion. The way I was taught is that there are two types of risotto: those that take their flavor solely from a spice and a broth, and those that, in addition to a cooking broth, also call for a base. Once both of these techniques have been honed, a risotto can be made with pretty much anything. It is the ingredients before you that will determine how.

Many of us have perhaps been taught to use a soffritto as a base flavoring. As we have seen with soup, a soffritto indeed has its merits, but I do not recommend it for risotto. The dance of risotto is in mastering the rhythm and momentum at which the rice releases its starch. A soffritto gets in the way, it crowds the pan, treads on your toes—there is no joy in driving a racing car through heavy traffic. The entire flavor that a soffritto would impart can be just as easily isolated and seasoned into a base.

A base discreetly carries the flavor of the risotto's star ingredient from within and allows the garnish to take center stage upon serving. Whilst preparing the garnish for a risotto of mushrooms, for instance, you will accumulate trimmings, stalks, and less noble-looking specimens that can be recycled. Sauté these leftovers with a finely diced onion and gently simmer them to taste in a shallow covering of broth with sage and juniper; having seasoned this concoction to your palate, then blend it into a base which you will add little by little throughout the cooking of the rice. It will give heart to the flavor of your dish. Separately, you will have sautéed and seasoned the mushrooms just so and elegantly prepped them into bite-size morsels for garnish.

A spring risotto calls for a vegetable base. Use whatever offcuts you have, again sautéed and simmered in broth, then seasoned and puréed. A base of asparagus stalks, peas, and mint for instance. Perhaps bulk it up with an onion and a leek. Simmer to taste, then grind through a vegetable mill with an herb that enjoys a natural synergy with the lead ingredient: the green beard of fennel to accentuate peas or asparagus, tarragon for carrots, dill for broad beans, parsley for artichokes.

A clam risotto might inspire you to improvise a base by gently simmering a fine dice of onion and parsley with an anchovy fillet. A ladle of clam broth to deglaze, and swift passage through a vegetable mill, and you'll have a base condiment, to add—to taste—as the rice cooks.

A saffron risotto, on the other hand, calls for no more than a good broth. Saffron is water-soluble and will impart its flavor to the rice effortlessly. The same applies to an oyster risotto, as we shall see in the upcoming recipe. It is enough for the rice to be flavored by a shellfish broth, with the oysters added at the very last moment, to lightly poach before you in the heat of the rice.

The same applies to an herb risotto; these are simple dishes, where you will cook the rice with a spice and an aromatic in a seasoned broth. There are many qualities of risotto rice, from the artisanal to the industrial. And several varieties, Vialone Nano, Arborio, and Carnaroli are the best known. Vialone Nano holds its starch well and is a particular favorite of those who aspire to cook rice al dente.

Be under no illusion as to the industrial scale of the farming methods employed in the production of risotto rice. As I write this, I have just come back from cooking in Milan and an early morning drive through the rice fields of the Po Valley was eye opening. There are organic and natural rice products on the market: gravitate towards these. There is even vintage risotto rice, air-dried and aged. It will set you back ten dollars a pound and is worth every cent.

Once you have carefully selected your preferred variety of rice it still faces the journey from larder to plate. The first step is to add the dry rice to a hot pan, with a small knob of butter and a bay leaf. Move the rice around until it is too hot to hold in the hand. Toasting the rice in this manner enables greater control over the release of starch. The next step is the addition of white wine. Given the heat, the wine will be absorbed instantly, imparting a degree of acidity to the outer skin of the rice. This will provide balance to the oncoming addition of fat.

Broth or water, salted to one and a quarter teaspoons per quart (seven grams per liter), now needs to be added ladle by ladle throughout. Risotto requires your total attention. The rice must be just covered with broth at all times: never so much as to slow the momentum of the cooking, and just enough to have it on the verge of wanting a little more.

Stir constantly in a gentle action, moving the rice at the bottom of the pan to the top. A little base should be added just after the first covering of broth to qualify the dish to come. The importance of tasting constantly as you go cannot be overstated—it will direct you in the timing of when to add more base *bit by bit*. Keep in mind that if you inundate the rice with a surplus of base, it will prematurely cause the emulsion to thicken and hinder the rice's capacity to release starch.

A good way to master the steps to cooking a proper risotto is to start with risotto alla parmigiana. It is how apprentices are taught in restaurants. This is a plain risotto made with no base and finished with grated Parmesan, butter, and olive oil, which are added once the pan is off the heat. This exercise illustrates clearly to the novice how the rice releases its starch unhindered. See recipe, page 147.

Having garnered a feeling for this, to then judge the quantity of base to be added at any given moment during the cooking of a garnished risotto soon becomes second nature. The rule of thumb: just enough to add body and umami, never enough to hinder the controlled release of starch.

Continue this way, adding broth ladle by ladle until the rice is deemed *almost* al dente. Which is to say, the precise moment it is cooked *almost* to perfection. With practice you will learn to recognize the quality of "undercooked" that is required at this stage. We want it undercooked because two steps still remain to finish the risotto: *la mantecatura* and the adjusting of heat and consistency.

Take the almost al dente rice off the heat and execute what in Italian is called *la mantecatura*, which is to say the addition of seasonings and fat in the form of butter, olive oil, herbs, grated Parmesan, and according to the type of risotto, perhaps base. *La mantecatura* requires a particular stirring action; with practice you will soon get the knack of it. Hold the spatula in your right hand so it is an extension of your forearm. With your other hand, tilt the rice pan forward and slide it back and forth in a controlled motion. Thus thoroughly mixing rice, oil, and base, incorporating air as you go. You are stirring, but in fact it is the pan that is moving back and forth, whilst your stirring arm remains motionless. For want of a better description, you want the spatula to work as a paddle systematically cresting a wave through the pan.

The objective of *la mantecatura* is to form an emulsion between starch, fat, and broth. The reason this is performed off the heat is that, should the temperature be too high when adding butter, the fat will boil, the emulsion will split, and all your efforts will have been in vain.

Add olive oil and or butter, base, grated cheese if you desire, and season the rice to taste. Add the garnish and fresh herbs, then put the pan back on the stove and carefully—avoid boiling—bring the finished risotto back up to serving temperature.

Adjust the consistency by adding more broth to stretch the emulsion if necessary. The optimum consistency is *all'onda*: the risotto forms a cresting wave when the pan is tugged stridently backwards.

You might garnish a tomato risotto with basil flowers, a pumpkin risotto with roasted spatchcocked quail. A rosemary risotto with stewed shank of veal, an asparagus risotto with seared sea scallops, a parsley risotto with sautéed veal kidneys—the list is infinite. Risotto makes a great dish for a small dinner party. That is, if you can abandon your guests for the twenty minutes it takes to cook one. The secret to risotto is to master the method and then improvise.

Cooking Spaghetti

A common mistake made by amateur pasta cooks is to be stingy with water. Pasta contains starch, and needs to be cooked in abundant salted water at a rolling boil. If the volume of water is insufficient, starchy, stewed noodles ensue. So equip yourself with a large saucepan (you will find all sorts of uses for it). There are even those designed specifically for cooking pasta, garnished with a double colander that enables you to lift the pasta out of the boiling water in one gesture.

Spaghetti alla chittara is a personal preference. Instead of being rounded, they are squared, elongated rectangular lengths with four flat sides, upon which sauce effortlessly finds footing. They come in a standard generous gauge not dissimilar to that of spaghettoni. That is to say thick, needing a good ten minutes to cook in fast boiling well-salted water.

I was taught at Harry's Bar that properly cooked pasta should be cooked "dry on the plate, wet in the mouth." It is a mantra, somewhat cryptic, but that nevertheless makes sense in practice and to which I adhere. You do not want pasta swimming in sauce. Rather you want bite. Pasta al dente means neither undercooked nor overcooked, but just so. Pasta upon which sauce has hitched a ride, forming an emulsion of the starch, fats, and broths contained therein. Just as there is a sleight of hand to be picked up and practiced for *la mantecatura* of risotto, so there is a knack to sautéing pasta.

The first tip is to choose the right pan. A high-sided pan with a good, long, preferably convex iron handle will help. Practice with dry rice in a pan; it is like tossing an omelet or a pancake. The forearm stays locked at the elbow, and moves from the shoulder with a flick of the wrist.

The sautéing action allows you to distribute heat evenly to the ingredients in the pan. Over a high flame, *sauté-sauté* and the ingredients from the bottom of the pan are brought to the top. This method allows you to condense flavors and to fine-tune the consistency (the aforementioned wetness) of your sauce.

A forkful of spaghetti alle vongole should leave the plate neatly and release layers of flavor as it is bitten into: parsley freshly chopped, clam juice absorbed into the pasta, sweet succulent clams (or sweeter still cockles), and black pepper. Season depending, there might also be the peppery kick of new season olive oil. The objective is always dry on the plate, wet in the mouth. This is achieved by finishing the pasta in its sauce over a fierce flame during the last ninety seconds or so of cooking.

Cooking pasta should be considered as a three-pronged attack. The first thing is cooking your pasta al dente. Meanwhile you will have concocted an emulsion of your sauce in a pan, into which you will transfer the al dente pasta. Then you bring the pasta and sauce together, seasoning as you go. The key lies in adopting a winning attitude, in the timing, and in projecting a clear vision of the task ahead. There is an Italian saying, *ci vuole coraggio per coucere la pasta* (cooking pasta calls for courage).

As for fresh pasta, if you want to make it from scratch, wonderful. So-called fresh pasta picked up in a packet, on the other hand, is not worth the cellophane it is wrapped in. At Harry's Bar, pasta was crafted all day, every day. It is a practical and economical way of recycling scraps and morsels. Italian restaurants enjoy the advantage of being able to recycle and sell the same ingredient a number of times. Lobster tail as salad, lobster "bits" as ravioli. In Italy, if you are lucky enough to happen upon dough kneaded by a grandmother's hand, fresh tagliolini, ravioli, tagliatelle, tortellini *e tuti quanti* are without doubt food in the vernacular and delightful.

Risotto alla Parmigiana

This is the simplest of all risottos and therefore by definition one of the trickiest to perfect. Any two cooks will conjure quite different results. Like all simple dishes, it allows the sleight of hand and the palate of the individual cook to shine through, or—as the case may be—stand exposed as an ogre and coward hiding behind the sheen of butter.

A Parmesan (or pecorino) risotto is judged on the quality of the base ingredients and the lightness of hand employed in bringing them together into a homogeneous and umami-filled plate of rice. Focus is on the degree to which the rice is cooked, to the flavor imparted to the dish by the choice of broth, and lastly, to the quality (and quantity) of the butter and cheese used in *la mantecatura*.

Aim to master all of the different steps to cooking a risotto. This plain broth-based recipe illustrates clearly to the novice just how rice releases its starch. Practice makes perfect, so get the knack of each different step. Once you have the technique down and get a feeling for rice and starch, and for working an emulsion, you will start to have fun and improvise.

You might use mineral water, chicken broth, beef consommé. Or pecorino, a sheep cheese of higher flavor than Parmesan. You might omit butter for olive oil, or use a mixture of both. Once you have mastered the method you will be free to be led by your own palate and imagination.

INGREDIENTS
—*Serves 4*

1 ⅓ cups (280g) risotto rice
A small knob of butter to toast the rice
Bay leaves
2 oz. (60ml) white wine
4 ¼ cups (1l) of broth, or water, salted to ⅓ tsp/cup (7g/l)
Butter, detailed into knobs and chilled
Extra virgin olive oil
Grated Parmesan, or pecorino
Fleur de sel
Black pepper

Risotto allo Zafferano

Saffron risotto has firm footing in the camp of broth risotti. For this dish, you will need quality rice, saffron of known provenance, and mineral water, vegetable broth, or chicken broth. If following the iconic recipe to the letter, you would use veal consommé to cook the rice, and roast bone marrow for *la mantecatura*. Copious amounts of chilled butter and grated Parmesan cheese are often (though unnecessarily) added to saffron risotto; *riso Milano* is the kitchen vernacular for this dish.

Saffron risotto is one of the great staples of the Northern Italian kitchen. As fate would have it, I was introduced to Gualtiero Marchese recently in Milan. A guiding light of Italian cookery, a chef now nearly ninety years old, he has trained a generation of Italian chefs (now mostly in their fifties and sixties), under some of whom I have had the fortune to cook. Within half an hour of us sitting together, he had summoned forth a saffron risotto. The next day I found myself in the kitchen of another Milanese institution well after midnight, after having myself served a banquet of finger food to hundreds of people. The chef's welcome was a grand tour of the larders to admire the produce, whereupon a prosciutto-carving contest spontaneously broke out and bottles of fine white wine were enthusiastically opened—just in case—as spaghetti al pomodoro was served for the whole kitchen brigade. This denotes the convivial identity-affirming sense of Italian homecoming associated with pasta and risotto, inclusive to all, even those merely Italian in spirit.

It is said that saffron is a mild mood-enhancing hallucinogen. Its euphoric and aphrodisiacal aura may be the result of its exquisite color, like that of the life-giving sun. It has a faintly bitter yet sweet and hay-like flavor. It is the most expensive spice in the world by weight, so beware of being swindled. The stigmas of saffron crocuses are picked by hand, one by one, hence the price. Avoid powdered saffron and choose traceable stigmas.

INGREDIENTS
—*Serves 4*

1 ⅓ cups (280g) risotto rice
A small knob of butter to toast the rice
Bay leaves
2 oz. (60ml) white wine
4 ¼ cups (1l) of broth, or water, salted to ⅓ tsp/cup (7g/l)
Saffron stigmas
Butter, detailed into knobs and chilled
Extra virgin olive oil
Grated Parmesan, or pecorino
Fleur de sel
Black pepper

Organize all of your ingredients before you: rice measured out accordingly. Parmesan freshly grated. Butter (if you are going to use it), detailed into thumb-size cubes and reserved in the refrigerator. (It is important to chill the butter so it immediately reduces the

temperature of the rice when the butter enters the pan, thus optimizing *la mantecatura*.) Bring the broth or mineral water up to a simmer. Have saffron at hand, and commence.

Begin by toasting the rice and adding the wine as described in the introductory notes (page 143). Now add your first ladle of broth and stir in a gentle motion moving the rice at the bottom of the pan to the top. There are those who first dissolve the saffron stigmas in a ladle of hot broth before adding them, and others who add them directly to the rice. Whichever your chosen method, now is the time to add a few stigmas, imparting a base flavor to the rice and awakening the eye to the sunlit color of the dish to come.

Continue to add the broth or water ladle by ladle so that the rice is just covered with broth at all times. Taste as you go: a pinch more saffron, salt perhaps? Be warned that the flavor of saffron has a salty quality to it (as does Parmesan) and so be measured with your seasoning.

There is no such thing as the right amount of saffron to add. Rather, pitch the degree of flavor and color to your mind's eye and palate by adding it little by little.

When you deem the rice to be *almost* al dente, it is time to perform *la mantecatura*. Take the pan off the stove and tilt it forward with a spatula in one hand and the pan's handle in the other. Energetically stir the rice in a back and forth movement to aerate it and reduce the temperature. Then add a knob or two of chilled butter, and stir some more.

The elasticity of the emulsion is stretched with the addition of broth, and tightened with the addition of cheese. If you feel the consistency of the rice is too tight, add a little broth. If, on the contrary, it seems too loose, add some grated Parmesan. Olive oil, cheese, and butter are the fats that bind the broth and starch. All of these ingredients carry flavor, and the relative proportion of each will affect the success of the finished dish. Ultimately you want just the right amount, so proceed with specificity. Be clear beforehand in your mind's eye how you want the dish to taste. The emulsion should be tight yet malleable.

Working quickly, taste and season the rice to your palate. Perhaps add a grating of Javanese pepper or a pinch of saffron. Place the pan upon the stove once more. Bring it up to temperature by adding half a ladle of broth to perfect the *all'onda* consistency, so that the rice crests a wave in the pan when tugged stridently backwards. And serve. Dispense with laying the table with grated Parmesan or pepper: people reach for these by reflex, and ruin delicately seasoned food.

Risotto Ostriche e Prezzemolo

Risotto with oysters and parsley is a very simple dish best eaten in winter, when oysters are at the height of their season and valiant parsley stands tall in the face of bitter frost. This is a broth risotto, meaning it requires no base. The oysters themselves will yield some liquid, but not much. Filter and reserve whatever liquor they offer up; you will add it

when landing the dish as you bring the risotto back up to temperature, thus serving the subtle and volatile flavor of oyster liquor to the table.

For the best result, make a shellfish broth by steaming open cockles, mussels, or clams in half an inch of mineral water. Filter the resultant broth through muslin. The shellfish themselves can be used for a salad or finger food. For this recipe it is their liquor that we want for broth. Homegrown parsley is an immediate upgrade. If it is cut from a plant that is a couple of years old, better still. The stalks, bound together with string, will flavor the rice as it cooks. Finely chop the fragrant leaves and any bolting sprigs you are lucky enough to find and add just prior to serving.

If you fear that you are short on shellfish broth, organize a pan of mineral water with bay leaves and parsley stalks. Bring this up to a simmer to infuse, and hold it in reserve as backup.

INGREDIENTS
—*Serves 4*

1 ⅓ cups (280g) risotto rice
A small knob of butter to toast the rice
Bay leaves
2 oz. (60ml) white wine
4 ¼ cups (1l) of shellfish broth, or water, salted to ⅓ tsp/cup (7g/l)
Two dozen oysters, shucked and their strained liquor reserved
A bunch of parsley
The deseeded flesh of a mild chili
Extra virgin olive oil
Fleur de sel

Once you have all the ingredients laid out before you, commence. Proceed just as you did for the previous recipe but replace the saffron with parsley stalks, bay leaves, and the deseeded flesh of half a mild chili. These are to be changed as and when you see them losing their chlorophyll sheen. The chili as soon as it has made its point can be lifted out and discarded.

Cook the rice to almost al dente, adding the shellfish broth ladle by ladle as you go. A very fine dice of the more tender parsley stalks can be slipped in quite early on to establish a base note of parsley. These will disappear into the rice.

Take the pan off the stove with the rice wet, but not swimming in broth. Judge the moment you take the pan off the stove with an eye to the desired consistency of the finished dish. In this instance, you will use no cheese (never with fish), nor any butter to help you tighten the rice, as the emulsion will be made with olive oil. You *could* make an herb butter and use that instead of olive oil. But there is little reason to, other than gluttony, as a risotto without butter will better showcase the flavor of its star ingredient, and is both cleaner tasting and lighter to digest. Take the pan's handle in one hand and a spatula in the other and in the now familiar way, energetically stir and aerate the rice. Add olive oil and finely chopped parsley and stir some more. Finally add the shucked oysters. Check the seasoning for salt and return the pan to the stove. Adjust the consistency with the oyster liquor previously set aside so the rice crests a wave in the pan, *risotto all'onda*.

Risotto al Granchio

Quite distinct from taste (sour, salty, umami, bitter, and sweet, which are perceived on the top of the tongue by the taste buds), flavor is aromatic, volatile, and ephemeral. It is picked up by the olfactory nerves on the roof of the palate and anticipated by the nose once fixed upon by the eye. Crab is an ingredient well endowed with both taste and flavor. The taste of the crab resides in the dark meat of the head shell, and its flavor in the delicately textured white meat. Herein lie both base and garnish.

In "Savory First Courses," we explored how to best cook and transform crab into three textures: white meat, dark meat, and broth. The white meat will be your garnish to add during *la mantecatura*. The dark meat will provide the base, which you will add throughout the cooking in accordance to taste.

INGREDIENTS
—*Serves 4*

A 2 to 3 lb. (1kg) hen crab for dark meat
A 2 to 3 lb. (1kg) cock crab for white meat
1 ⅓ cups (280g) risotto rice
A small knob of butter to toast the rice
Bay leaves
2 oz. (60ml) white wine
4 ¼ cups (1l) of shellfish broth, or water, salted to ⅓ tsp/cup (7g/l)
Fleur de sel
Extra virgin olive oil
The beard and young shoots of a Florence fennel, finely diced
Tender leaves of chervil, tarragon, and parsley

Cook the crabs as per the instructions for "White & Brown Crab Salad" (page 119).

To make the base, first check the dark meat for errant cartilage, shell, or other unsavory bits. Chop it finely and pass it through a sieve. To organize the garnish, pick the white meat from the claws and legs. Then gently simmer a broth from the skulls in mineral water.

Place the risotto pan onto the stove over a medium flame and add a couple of bay leaves and a small knob of butter. Toast the rice and quench it with a glass of wine, in the now customary manner. Now add a ladle of broth, just enough to cover the rice. Stir and taste. Correct the seasoning for salt. Add a little of the brown crabmeat to qualify the risotto. Continue cooking the risotto as previously described. Taste regularly so as to gauge when to add more base. It should be just enough to add body and umami, never enough to hinder the controlled release of starch. Keep going until the rice is *almost* al dente. Combine all the ingredients to create a successful emulsion at *la mantecatura*, using the particular turn of hand and stirring action that you have by now perfected. Take the pan off the heat and start stirring to incorporate air into the rice and reduce the temperature to slow the cooking. Whilst constantly stirring, add brown crabmeat and taste. Add olive oil. Add finely chopped young shoots of fennel for texture and taste. Add half of the herbs and half of the white meat, and stir some more. Correct the seasoning. Return the pan to the heat and adjust the consistency with more broth *all'onda*. Transfer the risotto to a warmed serving dish and garnish with the remaining white meat, fennel beard, chervil, parsley, and tarragon.

Risotto Pomodoro, Mozzarella di Bufala, Fiori di Basilico

This is a favorite with kids. When both tomatoes and basil are abundant it is an easy dish to cook for a hungry summer table. It is a risotto made with a base of tomato sauce, a *passata*.

For the broth, your choice should be tailored to your palate and to the occasion. Chicken broth will give a hearty umami result. Mineral water brought to a simmer with bay and chili is usually more than satisfactory and gives the tomato, basil, and fresh mozzarella a clean platform upon which to express themselves.

High-season cherry tomatoes, harvested from under the August sun, make delightful garnish for this dish. If they are industrial imposters grown with their roots in artificial nutrient- and saline-fed beds, then picked green, rinsed in chlorine, and shipped in packets, better to skip them altogether and change the menu. This dish is as good as the tomatoes, so focus on shopping and or gardening.

INGREDIENTS
—*Serves 4*

1 ⅓ cups (280g) risotto rice
A small knob of butter to toast the rice
Bay leaves
2 oz. (60ml) white wine
4 ¼ cups (1l) of broth, or water, salted to ⅓ tsp/cup (7g/l)
2 lbs. (900g) of sauce tomatoes, to yield half a pint (285ml) of passata
Basil
Cherry tomatoes, or dice of skinned and diced tomato flesh for garnish
Mozzarella di bufala, diced into fingertip sized bites
Extra virgin olive oil
Parmesan, or pecorino
Fleur de sel
Black pepper

Source mozzarella, made not with cow's milk but buffalo milk. Naples prides itself on the quality of its mozzarella. Source it fresh and chop it into bite-size pieces.

If you have cherry tomatoes, halve or quarter them and set them aside for the tomato garnish. Alternatively select sauce tomatoes, or plum tomatoes as they are sometimes called. Make a shallow crisscross incision to each tomato with a paring knife and briefly blanch them by dropping them in boiling water for half a minute followed immediately by an ice bath. Peel away the skin and halve, quarter, and eighth the tomatoes detailing them into an even sized dice.

If you have basil in the garden, pick a mixture of young fragrant leaf and bolting flowering stems. You might steep some of these flowering stems in olive oil for a few hours to concoct basil oil, which will greatly upgrade your weaponry of condiments when it comes to *la mantecatura*. Organize the basil into leaf and flower.

To make the base use sauce tomatoes like Roma, San Marzano, or any other similar variety. These have much lower water content than salad tomatoes. Chop them coarsely and put them in a pan over a lively heat with a bay leaf and a branch of flowering basil; add a little mineral water to get things started. Bring this up to a boil, and then simmer the sauce to taste. Pass it through a vegetable mill, and you are all set.

When you have all your ingredients before you, the cooking broth beside you on the stove at a gentle simmer, and garnished with a ladle, then commence. Cook the risotto in the usual way, tasting as you go. Adding a spoon of base here and there, changing the bay leaves and branches of flowering basil as needed. During *la mantecatura* add tomato base and olive oil, some butter if you wish, and stir. Add the diced tomato (or cherry tomatoes) and the mozzarella. Season with grated Parmesan or pecorino; bring the pan back to the stove, and perfect the consistency *all'onda* by adding broth or base, as your palate directs you. Add abundant chopped basil to the top of the risotto and serve it straight to the center of table.

Spaghetti alle Vongole

This is a dish to be eaten by the sea, or at least somewhere with access to a good fish market. If you are on a mountaintop, make spaghetti *bottarga* instead. People talk of chocolate being the food of the gods; forget it, spaghetti alle vongole any day. If I were to choose one dish over all others it would be this. There are many members of the mollusk family and they are all equally good. Tellini, small and shiny like well-polished fingernails, are a favorite. Cockles are a delicacy, with their variegated shells and sweet succulent flesh. Large clams are less tender and not such a hit. Small mussels such as *moules de buchot* are particularly good, pert and tasting of the sea. All these shells are prepped and cooked in just the same way, so go with what you can find.

When you buy them, be sure that all the shells are tightly shut. Those gaping ajar with faraway eyes are dead or dying and to be given a wide berth. People are known to do all sorts of strange things when it comes to cleaning clams, such as soaking them in saltwater to purge them of sand. Not a good plan, unless perhaps you do it in fresh seawater. It is enough to apply a couple of strokes of bristled brush where called for, and rinse them quickly and thoroughly so as to hold on to the taste of the sea. Place a colander in a large bowl, and empty the clams into the colander. Run a fast cold tap upon them and dance them about with your hand. Lift the colander up, and any sand there was should have settled at the bottom of the bowl. Repeat until the water runs clear.

INGREDIENTS
—*Serves 4*

8 oz. (240g) dry pasta: spaghetti alla chittara, spaghettoni, or linguine
2 lbs. (1kg) un-shucked clams
Mineral water
Bay leaves
A sprig of thyme

The deseeded flesh of a mild chili
Parsley
A clove of garlic
Extra virgin olive oil
Fleur de sel
Black pepper

Choose the aromatics you want to steam the shells open with. Bay, thyme, chili, and parsley perhaps, garlic if it is the season and it is fresh.

Choose a pan large enough to receive the shells without stacking them too high, and one that has a lid. (Alternatively, cook the shells in batches.) Heat the pan; add the aromatics and then a line of olive oil. In go the shells. Add half a ladle of mineral water to get things going and close the lid. The key is that the shells are heated evenly and open together. Retrieve them from the pan the moment they open.

Beside the stove, organize a muslin-lined sieve sitting upon a bowl to strain the steamed clams. Work quickly to separate three quarters of the clams from their shells. Rinse all the clams (including those still in the shell) in their broth, being sure to purge any errant sand. Then strain the broth once more.

You now have three components: broth, plus clams, both on and off the shell. The clams will be your garnish. The broth will be reduced over a high flame, and absorbed into the spaghetti, carrying flavor to the plate. It is the nectar that will make the dish.

Cook the spaghetti in abundant fast-boiling water salted to two teaspoons per quart (ten grams per liter). If the package indicates eleven minutes, set the timer for nine.

Set a large sauté pan over a medium heat and add the clam broth. Add thyme, chili, and bay, then a line of olive oil and a small knob of butter, and work these elements together into a loose emulsion, which will become your sauce.

Reduce if necessary, keeping in mind our mantra. Season the sauce to taste. Take out the chili once it has performed its task and change any herbs that lose their chlorophyll sheen.

Strain the pasta, add it to the pan and turn up the heat. Once the temperature penetrates the heart of the pan and the sauce starts to bubble, begin to sauté the pasta, bringing the bottom to the top around and around in a swift and rhythmic gesture. Then pin the pan's bottom straight back upon the flame to cook, reduce, and tighten further.

Continue to sauté your spaghetti and add the clams. Season with parsley, olive oil, and pepper, and sauté some more. Taste and once satisfied: *a tavola!*

Spaghetti al Pomodoro

Spaghetti al pomodoro, rather like risotto alla parmigiana, is a super simple dish that no two cooks will finish the same way. And it will be approached quite differently at different times of year, usually on a sliding scale of success, depending on the cook's own personal sensorial reference for ripe tomatoes picked from under the summer sun.

At the height of summer, a roughly chopped, freshly picked tomato tossed in white pasta is unbeatable. Make a light emulsion with a ladle of the pasta water, a line of olive oil, and a small knob of butter. Add a couple of thinly sliced cloves of new season garlic, a bay leaf, stalks of flowering basil and the flesh of a chili (a half or a quarter that you can retrieve once it has made its point). Work this around into a loose emulsion.

You might add a fillet of salted anchovy one day and lemongrass leaves the next. It is these little variations on simple dishes—improvisations on the theme of what have I got and what can I do with it—that bring life and spark to the kitchen. Simple archetypal dishes allow for infinite freedom of expression.

If you are using Roma, or San Marzano tomatoes (which have much lower water content), blanch them, skin them, and roughly chop them. If you are using salad tomatoes, which are packed full of liquid, first blanch and peel them—you will want to halve them and squeeze them—then leave them to drain in a colander. Sieve this juice and add it at the very last minute as you sauté, it will impart vitality to the flavor of the finished dish.

Drain the spaghetti; add them to the pan and *sauté-sauté*, ensuring the forearm stays locked at the elbow and moves from the shoulder with a flick of the wrist. Add roughly chopped tomato—and tomato water—and sauté some more. Correct the seasoning; add chopped basil, olive oil, and basil flower oil if you have it, sautéing the pan the whole way to table.

In winter you will reach into the larder for a jar of tomato sauce that you made in August or early September because no fresh tomatoes are available. There are none of any worth and vitality outside their short season.

Summer tomatoes ground through a tomato mill. This is an ingenious old-fashioned tool that separates tomato skin and seed from flesh. Garnished with a funnel-like opening to which one adds the tomatoes from above. You turn a handle, which turns a corkscrew contraption through a long perforated beak. The seed and skin are expelled through the end of the beak, and the tomato sauce cascades through its sides to be collected below. You will find one clamped to most Mediterranean kitchen tables through the latter part of August.

Any two cooks will process this resultant sauce, juice, or proto-passata in any number of ways. Whether turned into a hearty sauce with resort

to a soffritto, or flavored with different herbs and spices, each will refer to how they were taught, how their grandmothers did it, a homing response to the timeless sensorial world of childhood.

By far the simplest method is to bring the sauce up to a simmer and skim away the red scum that forms on its surface, as you would skim a broth. Continue until it runs clear. Then reduce the sauce to the consistency you desire. Keep in mind that many passata are rather thick, and the minute you heat them they will reduce and thicken further. Adding water seems pointless, so keep the passata suitably liquid. Once you are happy, turn off the heat and steep young fragrant tomato branches in the sauce to infuse. Organize sterilizing jars and fill them with sauce. Close them tightly. Weight them and submerge them in water, sterilizing them at 175°F (80°C) for an hour. Stock the larder with these for the winter.

Come winter, reach in and bring summer sun to the depths of your winter table. Finely dice an onion and put it to gently fry in a little oil with a bay leaf. Once translucent, add a jar of passata, bring it to a simmer and correct the seasoning to your palate. Cook the pasta al dente; add it to the sauce, and *sauté-sauté*. Add parsley or perhaps bolting sprigs of peppery rocket, whatever winter herbs you have to hand. If you have had the foresight to macerate basil in oil, or bay and chili, you might use these too. Again there are no rules, only what method enables and the palate aspires to.

Spaghetti alla Carbonara

Carbonara is classically composed of bacon, cream, eggs, and Parmesan. There are those who add sherry and other such audacious trimmings. My version is stripped down in the extreme. No dairy. Rather, a celebration of the natural affinity of pork to sage, onion to star aniseed, and parsley to egg.

INGREDIENTS
—Serves 4

8oz. (240g) dry pasta: spaghetti alla chittara, spaghettoni, or linguine
An onion
Star aniseed
Bay leaves
Thickly-sliced smoked streaky bacon, or pancetta
Sage
Olive oil
Chicken broth, or mineral water
An egg yolk or two
Nutmeg
Parsley
Chervil

Finely dice an onion with a razor-sharp knife. You want to optimize the texture of the onion so be sure not to bruise it as you cut. Organize an equal-sized dice of smoked streaky bacon, free of the rind.

Put a pan over a low flame and add a bay leaf, the bacon, the sage, a star aniseed, and very little olive oil. Gently fry the bacon to crisp, let it begin to color, then add the onion. The water content of the onion will subtly deglaze the pan and bring together the mildly caramelized flavors of sage, bacon, and aniseed. You might add a very fine dice of tender parsley stalks for another layer of flavor. As the onion becomes translucent, deglaze the pan with a shallow ladle of chicken broth or mineral water to stretch the emulsion and homogenize all the flavors into one. Reduce this slightly and then set it aside off the heat.

Separate a couple of egg yolks and whisk them in a bowl, together with their equivalent volume of chicken broth or mineral water. Grate some nutmeg into this mixture. Set aside a reserve of finely chopped parsley and chervil.

Boil the spaghetti two minutes short of the time indicated on the box. Drain it and add it to the pan of seasoned onion and bacon; *sauté-sauté*. Add parsley and chervil. Add the egg yolk and broth mixture and sauté some more. Work swiftly; the objective is for the egg yolks to bind the ingredients together into a rich and homogeneous sauce. You certainly do not want it to cook too long and congeal. Perfect the consistency by adding a little more broth if called for, and sauté the pasta all the way to table.

Eat it immediately! This is not a dish that waits.

Spaghetti con Bottarga

Bottarga is a larder condiment par excellence, one that shines Mediterranean sun into the depths of winter. Made of grey mullet eggs salted, dried, and preserved in beeswax, bottarga has not changed its look since antiquity. Hanging from a fishmonger's stand, it is a sight that can take you back in time. It would have looked precisely the same in Pompeii as it does today.

Rich and faintly salty, bottarga has an umami quality and heady flavor that keeps one reaching for more. Though it is used to garnish salads and makes a good seasoning for eggs, it is a delicacy with spaghetti. What's more, you can be at table in less than quarter of an hour.

INGREDIENTS
—*Serves 4*

8 oz. (240g) dry pasta: spaghetti alla chittara, spaghettoni, or linguine
3 ½ oz. (100 g) grated bottarga
Bay leaves
A knob of butter
Extra virgin olive oil

Put the pasta to boil and then focus on your sauce. Grate bottarga into a sauté pan. Add a ladle of water, a knob of butter, some olive oil, and a bay leaf. Over medium high heat, work these ingredients into a loose emulsion. Taste it and judge whether you need to add more bottarga.

Drain the pasta and add it to the pan and sauté. Grate more bottarga over the spaghetti and sauté some more. Taste as you go. Add more bottarga to tighten the emulsion, a shallow ladle of broth or water to stretch it out again.

Once you have the perfected the trinity of flavor, consistency, and al dente spaghetti, call everybody to table.

Spaghetti Aglio, Olio e Peperoncino

This is a recipe tailored to a bare larder, when all that remains is a clove of garlic, a chili pepper, and some olive oil. It is also one of the finest spaghetti dishes there is. It can be upgraded a little with the addition of a salted anchovy fillet, the pert flesh of a ripe tomato, and abundant parsley.

Again, success lies in assembling a savory emulsion of all the ingredients in such a way that their individual flavors are layered and distinguishable. The mistake many make with this recipe is that they add all the ingredients to the oil with no water—so they fry—and all the volatile fragrant qualities are compromised and embittered into a careless swill.

This is a dish that is naturally at its very best at the height of garlic season, when the bulb's water content is high and it has not yet formed the germ it would use to propagate itself anew.

INGREDIENTS
—Serves 4

8 oz. (240g) dry pasta: spaghetti alla chittara, spaghettoni, or linguine
A head of garlic, freed of its germ if out of season
A chili
A salted anchovy
Bay leaves
Parsley
Extra virgin olive oil
Fines herbes

Peel and slice the garlic very thinly indeed. As a result, it will cook quickly and curtail the need to heat the olive oil longer than necessary.

Wash a salted anchovy and detail it into fillets. Finely dice tender parsley stalks, and if it is summer, blanch and skin a tomato. Take a mild chili pepper and halve it along the vertical; with a filleting knife remove the fiery pith and seeds from within.

Put a sauté pan over the heat and add a generous covering of olive oil. Add the garlic, the parsley stalks, and the halved and deseeded chili. If you wish to add anchovy, add it now.

Very gently bring the garnished olive oil up to a simmer to optimize a fragrant infusion. As soon as the oil starts to bubble, add a shallow ladle of broth or mineral water. Shake the pan around in a circular motion to homogenize the emulsion. Season it to taste. You might take the chili out once it has done its job. And use a garlic squeezer to add more garlic if called for. Once content, remove the pan from the heat and stand its contents to infuse.

Cook the spaghetti al dente, drain it, and add it to the pan. *Sauté-sauté* and, depending on the season, add a dice of tomato, basil, parsley, or chervil, whatever you have to hand. Control the consistency by managing the elasticity of the emulsion in the usual way. Wild garlic leaves, or ramps as they are sometimes called, grow in woodland in late spring. These, roughly chopped and added at the very last moment, lift this dish to another realm.

SCALES & SHELLS

———— ✦ ————

BAKED BOTTOM FEEDERS

✳

POACHED FRESHWATER TROUT

✳

CHAR-GRILLED OILY FISH

✳

CITRUS-PICKLED WATER CREATURES

✳

ROAST BASS

✳

TEMPURA ROE

✳

SHARP EYES ON THE FISH COUNTER

Shopping for Fish

Fresh fish smells of the sea. Yesterday's fish smells of fish. If you happen upon a place where small boats come into harbor and sell the day's catch, enjoy it. There is no better place to buy it than at the source. Humble anchovy from this morning's nets makes for finer eating than yesterday's turbot. As mongers add value, vitality is diminished. Fish eaten within hours of being caught has a texture irreversibly lost thereafter.

Scales glisten and clear eyes stand convex. The color of gills betrays how long a fish has been out of the water. Look for brightly colored red. Flesh should pert to hand. A mucus layer known as a slime coat covers a live fish's outer body. This acts rather like our top layer of skin, as a first defense against disease and parasites. When shopping for fish look for glistening convex eyes and vibrant red gills, all smelling of the sea.

Alexandre Dumas Père mused in the nineteenth century that one could walk dry-shod across the Atlantic Ocean upon the backs of codfish. That was then. Wild fish are a major food resource, and stocks are in steep decline; those of large predatory fish are estimated to be down to around ten percent of their pre-industrial levels. Equate this with the subsequent increase in human population and do the math. Man is the most efficient predator the oceans have ever known. Industrial-scale fishing commenced in the 1950s, the global catch peaked in the 1980s, and today we are witnessing collapse of individual species; a spiral toward extinctions. Destructive trawling techniques are ever more ruthlessly efficient. Satellite-guided super-trawlers prowl far from home, violating the sea floor, disturbing the balance of local cultures and their economies. Setting up a global network of marine no-go zones could allow indigenous fish populations' environments to perpetuate.

Cage-farmed fish is as repellent as battery chicken. Much better getting your daily bread elsewhere: rice, lentils, corn, or potatoes with chili, green vegetables, soup—the staple diet that most of the world left to its own devices reaches to. Fish or meat is a treat, an add-on, not a given.

Farmed fish are caged together in large numbers and thus are vulnerable to disease and parasites; they are fed precautionary antibiotics to keep them alive. Non-renewable energy is used to harvest, transform, and then ship their feed across hemispheres. Several kilograms of wild anchovy ground into fishmeal create one kilogram of saleable-farmed salmon. When the stocks of wild anchovy are no longer sufficient to support this industry, what next? Recycled and sanitized industrial poultry manure seems a safe bet. These anemic, imprisoned salmon must have their feed spiked with paprika so as to color their flesh for the consumer's eye.

With a farewell to tuna, cod, and other prized predators, the underwater pecking order is up for grabs. Spiraling population explosions of promoted species; lobsters run riot until they are fished out of existence. Then the shrimp has his day, then the next in line, and so on down the food chain. With this in mind perhaps I should include recipes for jellyfish, plankton, and worms, casting a thought forward to an uncertain future.

Roasting Ocean Fish

Ask your fishmonger to leave the scales on. Tell him quickly; their reflex is to scale a fish immediately upon weighing it. In the heat of the oven the scales will melt, forming an outer shell. This will envelop the flavor and succulence of the flesh as it cooks.

Fish demand thorough cleaning. Remove the gills and guts. Any trace of gill or intestine that is left lurking in the stomach cavity would introduce bitterness to the pan juices to come. Invest in a good strong pair of fish scissors; they'll last generations.

Garnish the stomach cavity with branches of herbs, inserted so the stalks stick out of the fish's mouth. Tend towards the savory; these can be quite coarse, such as wild fennel, bay, or herbs that have bolted beyond all description of tenderness. Avoid using young delicate fines herbes; these will sweat, create steam, impede roasting, and oxidize to bitter in the heat of the oven.

Be sure to choose a generous-sized roasting dish, for if it is too small steam will be created around the edges, and impede roasting. Build a nest in the roasting dish with branches of bay, wild fennel, and whatever you have to hand. If you have no herbs it is better by far to line the bottom of the roasting pan with humble grease-proof paper than resort to vegetables. These again would sweat, create steam, and impede roasting.

Now stand the fish in swimming position, tummy flaps out, belly side down upon its nest of herbs. Do not bother with salt, no more than a sparse seasoning of the stomach cavity, keeping mind's eye and palate projected forward to the pan juices to come.

Pre-heat the oven to maximum, full blast. Place the fish into this blistering furnace for 8 minutes per pound (17 minutes per kilogram), or until just done. A fish taken out of the oven cooked to perfection will proceed to overcook in its accumulated temperature. So *undercook fish*, and allow it to rest.

Insert a knife through the skin that runs along the fish's back and you will see to what degree the flesh comes away from the bone. The ideal is that it *almost releases* from the bone. If it is any further advanced than that it requires immediate undressing and filleting from the bone to halt it cooking any further.

Roasting fish standing up in this way allows for very even cooking. As the scales have melted and become one with skin, they peel away whole, exposing the naked fillets. These can be lifted in very few gestures. Dress a warmed serving dish with the filleted fish and cover it in muslin. Muslin or absorbent kitchen paper holds temperature whist letting steam escape, thus halting the cooking process.

Time now to conjure a sauce. Return the head and bones to the roasting pan and pound them with the tail of a rolling pin. Add fresh herbs, mineral water, or fish broth. Bring this up to rolling simmer over a lively heat and adjust the seasoning to your taste. Emulsify with a whisk and a little olive oil and then strain the juice through a fine sieve directly over the filleted fish. Flatfish do not have scales. Massage them with olive oil before roasting. This will help the skin crisp a little and facilitate its removal for filleting. They have fins on either side of their bodies. Remove these with the aforementioned fish scissors, exposing the flesh along your cutting line. This will enable easy undressing. The offcuts are rich in gelatin and should roast in the pan beside the fish with forethought to the sauce to come.

Poaching Fish

Make a court bouillon (a short broth)—meaning make an infusion of aromatics, herbs, and vegetables in a quantity of water sufficient to receive the whole fish in swimming position.

Fennel, bay, star aniseed, these are classic choices of aromatics for court bouillon. Half an onion, a carrot, and a bulb of Florence fennel, add these to your fish kettle. Escoffier, and indeed generations since, would add wine; this is perceived as the done thing. Not I. At a push, perhaps a splash of herb flavored vinegar, tarragon, horseradish, or bay. But you are much better off using these condiments to qualify the accompanying sauce. As for the wine, if it is good, it will taste better in a glass. Herb- and vegetable-infused lightly salted water is the way; keep it clean.

Use whatever you have to hand. If you have bay leaves, an onion, and a carrot, you are already halfway there. If I am poaching a rainbow trout, I might simply use streamside aromatics such as wild fennel, wild garlic, and bay. Starting in cold water bring these aromatics up to a gentle simmer, and continue to simmer until the infusion is of desired intensity. Salt the court bouillon to taste. Increase the heat to a rolling boil, immediately add the fish, and turn off the heat.

If you have judged the size of your pan to the size of your fish, then the addition of the cold fish will reduce the water temperature down to optimal poaching territory of around 175°F, (80°C). You can verify and maintain this temperature with the help of a thermometer. Visually, if you see bubbles rising from the pan's bottom, then the water is too hot. The immediate temperature change will obviously vary according to proportions of water to fish. Have one fish kettle for salmon, and another for trout.

Gently poach for five minutes to the pound. Checking with a scalpel-like incision along the fish's back to catch the moment when the flesh just releases from the bone. For a big fish, you might add ice cubes to reduce temperature, and then let the fish cool awhile in the poaching broth before removing it. This will make moving the fish much easier. A hot, big, poached fish is liable to fall apart. And remember, to poach is to poach, not to boil. The operative word here is *gently*.

Large fish such as wild sea trout can be cooked in advance, perhaps even a number of them in batches, enabling you to prepare fish cooked to perfection for great numbers. A potato salad seasoned with chives, dill, and champagne. Cucumbers doused with tarragon vinegar, abundant mayonnaise, and herb flower salads. This is how to elegantly feed fifty people out of a kitchen the size of a postage stamp.

Shopping for Shellfish

Shellfish should be purchased alive and should be reactive to touch. Once out of the water, live shellfish survive on bodily reserves. Purchase a specimen that has hung around a moment too long and you'll be purchasing an empty and withered shell. Lobster and crab should snap at you. Oysters and scallops should be firmly shut tight and smelling of the sea. Avoid cockles, mussels, and clams with faraway eyes whose shells gape ajar. Prawns should be translucent and hop like crickets. Once home, store shellfish for the briefest time in a box placed on a cool floor in the dark, covered in a dishcloth scattered with ice.

Cooking Crabs & Lobsters

Plunge live crabs standing upright, toes first, into abundant boiling water salted to two tablespoons per quart (thirty-five grams per liter), which emulates seawater. Immediately turn off the heat and poach them at 175°F (80°C), counting ten minutes to the pound. Just as for lobster when the soft gelatinous bone of the pincer can be pulled from the claw, clean of meat, it is sure sign the crab is cooked.

Separate claws, legs, and heads into groups. Remove the shell from the head. Retrieve the dark meat, and possibly the coral too—that is, if the crabs are female and are at the point in their yearly cycle where they are building up to lay eggs. With scissors, remove the lungs that run along either side of the skull. And start picking the meat with an angled skewer. Picking crab is an exercise in patience rewarded by quality grazing. If the skull defeats you, place it into a small pan, cover it with mineral water, and simmer this to broth.

For lobster, plunge them alive, head first, into boiling water for a brief minute to kill them. Fish them out with a spider and separate them into four: rip the head off the tail, the pincer claws from the head, and, with scissors, chop off the legs. Reserve the head aside. Take a long skewer and carefully slide it between the armored shell and the tail. Section by section, uncurl the tail as you go; the lobster tail will thus cook straight, rather than curl. At 175°F (80°C), poach the tails for three minutes, the claws for two, and the legs for just one.

Just as soon as they are cooked refresh them in iced water. Remove the shell from the head; with sharp scissors remove the lungs. They run either side of the skull like great sprouting exhaust pipes mounted upon the cylinders of a powerful engine. Bash the lobster's skull to a pulp with the tail of a rolling pin. Collect and transfer the pulp to a small saucepan, cover it with mineral water, and simmer lobster broth to taste.

Cooking Clams, Cockles & Mussels

Start with a line of oil, a bay leaf, and sprigs of parsley. Flavors to qualify a hot pan, one with a tight-fitting lid. You can use lemongrass, ginger, and chili, whatever you wish.

Add the shellfish, a ladle of mineral water, and close the lid. Raise the heat to full blast and with a hand to the lid and the other to the pan's handle, shake every thirty seconds or so until the shells have opened. This will take barely a couple of minutes.

Take care to cook quantities in small batches, allowing you to cook the shells to the very moment they open, and no longer. The benefit in texture and flavor that working in such a controlled and specific manner achieves stands tall.

And if the zealous cocktail bore turns up, juggling wine and cream and curry powder all whilst trying to put his oar in and turn up the heat, politely suggest he lay the table instead.

If you are eating clams, cockles, or mussels as a meal unto itself, you may wish to bulk this up; gently fry a finely diced shallot or two with aromatics that will deglaze to a loose emulsion upon the addition of the shells. Serve a huge central bowl to the table garnished with a ladle; spelt bread to dip into the sauce. And soup spoons to drink up every last drop.

Baked Bottom Feeders

Flatfish feed predominantly along the ocean floor and as such are called bottom feeders. They wear both their eyes upon one side of the head, some to the left others to the right, with protruding eyelids, in the vein of the retractable electric headlights found on antiquated futuristic sports cars.

The underside skin is pale, smooth, and sleek. The upper side varies greatly, often cleverly equipped for purposes of subterfuge and hunting with a chameleon-like capacity to adjust pigmentation.

They come in all sizes, from huge Atlantic halibut to baby sole. Flash grilled, these are a delicacy. After halibut, in terms of size, come turbot, accepted by many as the king of the sea, for its fine texture and delicate flavor. Then come brill, plaice, and sole.

The firm texture of the flesh that holds its form through cooking is what singles out sole and turbot from the rest and makes them the most expensive by weight. If you happen upon a harbor where small boats come in, it is rather the freshness of the catch that will be the defining quality. Should there be turbot, the fisherman focused on selling his catch will do so at a price that sells.

For large turbot or plaice you might want to have the fish filleted or attempt it yourself. Season them well; you may in time organize yourself a shaker of salt, seasoned for grilling fish. Mix together in a mortar and pestle, coriander seeds, white peppercorns, a sprinkling of five bays; and work these into a dust. Combined together with fine sea salt to taste. Season the fillets and massage them with very little olive oil, then sear and mark them on a hot grill or in a metal handled nonstick pan. Transfer the pan to the oven for a short and sharp blast to cook through. Set the fillets aside to rest.

Halibut can be enormous, much larger than ovens (the record is in the region of a quarter of a ton) so there is little choice but to resort to knives. The same applies to large turbot: if the fish is more than a couple inches thick, cut generous sized steaks on the bone.

Cook them as above for fillets, starting them on top and then migrating the pan south to the oven, yet doubling the time in the oven, so the heat may penetrate through to the central bone. A couple of minutes on one side then turn the steak, and send it back to the oven for a couple of minutes more. The fish is cooked when it almost releases from the bone. It will rest to doneness in its accumulated temperature.

The method that yields the best results by far is to simply choose a fish of a size proportionate to the number of mouths to feed. For Valentine's Day, think a handsome turbot for two. If you are numerous, opt for the best specimens available, and roast these upon nests of herbs, counting a pound per person as described in the introduction to roasting ocean fish. If you spot brill, this is a good choice. It is just as delicate as turbot in flavor; the slightly less gelatinous texture is more than recompensed by the economy it offers to your purse.

Again you might serve brill with different accompaniments through out the year. Spring asparagus cooked as already described are pretty hard to beat. New potatoes peeled and dressed with dill. Wilted spinach and a tarragon mayonnaise.

Poached Freshwater Trout

Great-grandpa Oswald kept notes describing the meals he ate and the places he visited, including the different river fish he dined upon from region to region across France at the turn of the century. Such and such a fish would be "most highly esteemed" from such and such a river, according to the mineral qualities of the watershed along a river's path towards the sea. Such a sensorial journey is nowadays somewhat trickier. The rivers polluted and the creatures that lived in them extinct. Dams and overfishing having curtailed arrow-headed shoals of seasonal migrators. A few pike persist, terrorizing lake waters for frogs and duckling, perch, carp, and bream. Trout is farmed successfully, the higher the altitude the better. In any mountainous region with a steady supply of mineral spring water where there is no polluting upstream neighbor. Sturgeon for caviar is reared in such locations with increasing success; it has become the norm. Wild caviar is illegal, belonging to the past.

Rainbow trout, poached, served with braised fennel, and a watercress salad with horseradish sauce. This makes a clean flavored main course, for pre-winter.

INGREDIENTS
—*Serves 4*

2 rainbow trout
An onion
A carrot
Bay leaves
Wild fennel seeds
Star aniseed
Mineral water
Florence fennel
Olive oil
A large bunch of watercress
Horseradish sauce (page 129)

Choose a fish kettle suitably sized to fit the trout. Into this place an onion, a carrot, and a bulb of fennel, all halved along the vertical; bay leaves, wild fennel seeds, star aniseed, and the peelings of the horseradish that will become the accompanying sauce.

Cover these with mineral water and bring this up to a simmer. Continue to simmer the mixture until the desired depth of flavor is achieved. Then raise the heat ever so briefly to the boil. Add the fish, turn off the flame, and cover securely with a lid. Count five minutes to the pound and that's it.

The fish is cooked the moment it releases from the bone. With practice and care one gains a sense of timing. Again there is no set of strict instructions that will work at each instance. Much rather there is a way, a feeling, an instinct that can be learnt and honed with curiosity and time. This is true especially with fish cookery. Where the line between underdone and overcooked is crossed in a moment's inadvertence.

Halve, quarter, and eighth several bulbs of Florence fennel. Place a copper-bottomed pan over a moderate flame. Add a bay leaf, star aniseed, and a line of olive oil; work them around the pan with a spoon until the fat is impregnated with their scent.

Now add the fennel, gently coloring it briefly on each side. Add a shallow ladle of fish broth, or of court bouillon from the kettle; mineral water if you wish, and bring this to a fierce boil. Then swiftly cover the pan with a lid, to stand to rest, away from the heat in its accumulated temperature, to doneness.

As we have seen already in "Savory First Courses," horseradish sauce is easily made. The grating of the root will make your eyes water and clear the head. A job to delegate to the zealous; or guard for yourself if you are plagued by allergy or head cold. Take freshly finely grated horseradish root and add to this very little Dijon mustard. A splash of horseradish-flavored rice vinegar. Mix these to combine, and let them steep a few minutes. To finish the sauce, incorporate this mixture into a neutral mayonnaise, adjusting the consistency, if need be, with horseradish vinegar. Alternatively you may prefer to use crème fraîche. Very little is required, just enough to give body to your sauce.

Char-Grilled Oily Fish

Nowadays anchovies and sardines are caught in numbers to make fishmeal to feed their aquaculture brethren. It is one thing for a huge hungry salmon to gorge himself as he travels through a glistening shoal of anchovy, where they are fair game. It is quite different if the anchovy are caught under the floodlights of super trawlers equipped with satellite navigation. All to be ground, doctored, and fed to salmon residing thousands of miles away in cramped and parasite-ridden cages.

Fresh anchovies grilled over charcoal: a menu hard to beat. Accompany this with a high summer salad of raw sweet onion, basil, tomato, and white peach. An ice bucket garnished with a magnum of fair and dry rosé wine from the sun-kissed slopes of Provence. This is refined and distilled simplicity—true luxury.

INGREDIENTS
—*Serves 4*

2 dozen fresh anchovies

A SUMMER SALAD:
Large tomatoes
A couple of white peaches
A sweet salad onion
Abundant basil
Fleur de sel
Extra virgin olive oil

When grilling, intense dry heat is the goal—heat that will blister skin effortlessly. You manage the intensity of the cooking heat by moving the fish closer to or further away from the charcoal. Small terracotta grills are used in Morocco. Barely the size of a watermelon, opened in the form of an enormous soft-boiled egg. These are very practical, economical, and effective. The whole business can be seen to in less than half an hour.

Seaside fish restaurants that cater for great volume are equipped with huge grills mounted upon ratchets and pulleys. At noon they will be set high above the braise. And on throughout service the chef will gradually rack his grill down, so maintaining a constant and optimum grilling temperature throughout. As for all fish cookery, the objective is to catch the moment that flesh just releases from the bone.

Once the anchovies are cleaned, free of all trace of gut and gill, lay them out wearing their heads on absorbent paper to dry, and focus on your fire. Optimum grilling is achieved through the management of ember. It must neither be so high as to catch flame, nor emulate the enthusiastic reveler who despite best intentions peaks too early.

Oily fish such as sardine, mackerel, sea trout, and salmon are all well suited to grilling over fire; their inherent oiliness efficiently retains texture and succulence. You can of course grill whatever you wish, and you will find your own system and method. Flaky white fish however will rapidly and irreversibly dry out when carelessly grilled. Even tuna, swordfish, and fillets of bass, staples that folk barbecue; these enjoy several hours steeped in an olive oil based marinade prior to cooking.

Oily fish on the other hand are all set, ready to go. Just as the fish comes off the fire one can add an ephemeral layer of flavor. Great tall branches of wild fennel gathered in autumn and stored somewhere dry, thrust upon the embers to flare and send up wafts of aromatic smoke. Green fingered incense of sorts, which subtly impregnates blistered skin as it recoils from the heat. You can do this with rosemary or thyme, bay, indeed any aromatic herb prunings that you may have had the foresight to stash. Sage and lavender have the most purifying effect. If you are eating indoors and it's summer, the fire will not be lit. In the hearth burn a bunch of dried sage; it cleanses the energy of a room, like turning the page in a sketchbook. Nobody need know, yet the room will feel it.

Light your fire for grilling with kindling, small dry wood. And build it with deadwood of oak and ash, or any other slow burning non-resinous wood you have to hand. Build up a good heart, add charcoal, and stoke it. Once the flare has elapsed and you have a steady even glow, commence. This sounds perhaps obvious, though the napalm barbecue bunch have reflexes quite distinct, reaching to armories of petrol family aids. These ruin flavor, and defeat the object of the exercise, which is to celebrate the natural flavors of a given fish.

Citrus-Pickled Water Creatures

Tactics to optimize every last scrap and morsel of crabs and lobsters have been discussed. Savory first courses of succulent crustaceans, underscored with crisp textured vegetables, mildly tart fruit, and fines herbes. Delicate broths arisen from the extracted essence of pummeled and simmered skulls. Garnished with leftover scraps of meat hidden away in stray claws, discarded from a first sitting.

The mind's eye and palate are now also clear as to how to carefully steam open clams, cockles, and mussels in batches, just so, with the very minimum of fuss. All these creatures make good eating grilled. If you are on a beach at nightfall with a fire and yet no pot, this is your best bet. Take a live lobster and with a sharp knife halve it cleanly along the vertical in one controlled action. It will wriggle and thrash and have the uninitiated screaming.

Twist a knife between a crab's eyes and rip off its claws. Crack them and place them over the fire to grill. Many male crabs are caught just for their claws, and, as amputees, returned to the sea for the time it takes to grow a new set. Oysters placed over a fire will hold out until the adductor muscle can no more, then pop open. Eat them in one bite with a squeeze of lime.

A method of cooking that is celebrated in places where citrus fruit grow and fresh wild fish abound is ceviche. Any member of the bass family will happily lend itself to such treatment. That is the cooking, breaking down, denaturing of flesh through the addition of acids. Raw fish briefly marinated in citrus juice to cure awhile. Typically garnished with sweet raw onion for texture, the deseeded flesh of chili slivered into unobtrusive lengths for kick, and perhaps the lifted fillets from the citrus fruit itself.

This is a dish of assemblage rather than transformation. An abundance of choice cuts of raw fish seasoned with fragrant herbs to be eaten as it cooks. Granted, the citrus will have a denaturing and transformative effect upon the chosen fish, but the citrus too will have been chosen for its quality. You will have prepared all your ingredients separately and in advance. And only just prior to serving will you combine these and assemble the dish. Consequently the cooking effect of, say, lime is yours to judge. The longer it marinates the further cooked the fish will be. Time is the elastic; it's all about you. It is mind's eye and palate that bear the responsibility of calling this shot.

An assembled plate that is perfect now will be a sad affair twenty minutes hence. If this all sounds like too much palaver and you want something you can prepare in advance, skip ahead to the recipe for fish pie. It will be just as good, if you follow the line, and extract the essence of the component ingredients. And you can do this in peace over time.

Ceviche on the other hand requires you to pluck up the courage to perform center stage. Which is a perfectly straightforward proposal, as long as you are thoroughly prepared and organized. Once you have all the ingredients to hand, and the mouths to feed are in proximity, commence.

As with all structured improvisations the joy is to be found in exercising the unparalleled luxury of changing your mind as you go. Less chili for Molly, she's breastfeeding; no coriander for Etta; Louis wants oysters in his. How about using a little of that dipping sauce as a dressing? These wild nectarines are supremely tart, skip the lime segments and use these instead.

INGREDIENTS
—Serves 4

A lobster
4 live sea scallops
A deboned fillet of bass
4 oysters
A sweet salad onion
Lime fillets, or other citrus
Yuzu juice
A mild chili
A white peach
Bolting coriander

Kill lobster by method of choice. Do not poach the tail; rather undress it as it is, raw. A knife between the eyes and half an hour in the freezer is another option. And it will make taking the shell off much easier. Open live sea scallops by inserting a sharp blade into the mouth of the firmly shut shell. Force it ajar by turning the blade of your knife. Hold it in position with your thumb, as you slide the blade down the underside of the upper shell and sever the adductor muscle. Lift away the upper shell. With a spoon, retrieve the scallop discarding intestine and coral. The coral can be kept and dried—ground to a dust and used to bejewel seafood salads, pasta, and rice.

Clean the scallops under running water. They will probably wriggle so be warned. Slice the lobster tail into sashimi-size bites. And do the same for the scallop and the bass. The thinner the slices the quicker the effect will be of the oncoming citrus juice. It is a question of taste. I favor a thicker gauge giving a more textured bite.

Shuck oysters and reserve their juice in which you will rinse them, carefully eliminating errant shell, and set them aside in a bowl. Juice a lime or two. Or, if you're in luck, a yuzu, a particularly fine citrus fruit that is a hybrid of Chinese wild mountain lemon and mandarin. Lift the fillets from a couple more citrus fruit—lemon, lime, yuzu, tangerine, blood orange—with a razor-sharp knife, keeping an eye out for stowaway seeds.

Slice sweet summer onion to the size you desire. Organize a julienne of deseeded chili. Peel, half, quarter, and eighth the white peach or violet nectarine, whatever you're using. Select your herbs (bolting sprigs of coriander are pretty hard to beat), and then commence. There are no rules, rather just method applied to circumstance. It is supposed to be fun. Any combination of fish cut to the gauge you desire.

Roast Bass

Sea bass are insatiable hunters, feeding on smaller fish, crustaceans, and mollusks. Many species of bass exist, both freshwater and saltwater. From the almost extinct and deliciously gelatinous Chilean sea bass or Patagonian toothfish of the southern hemisphere north to the United States: the white bass of the West Coast and the striped bass of the East Coast. On across the Atlantic to Europe, sea bass is the name given. However in France and Italy those caught in the Mediterranean are called yet another name. In Italian, Adriatic Mediterranean and Aegean Sea bass are known as *branzino*, and those of the Atlantic *spigola*. In French the Mediterranean *bar* versus the Atlantic *loup-de-mer*, wolf of the sea, alluding to the fish's prowess as a hunter.

Whichever bass you happen upon, opt for the larger and wild line-caught specimen. Many tendered for sale are smaller and may have been industrially farmed. The ins and outs of which are alluded to in this chapter's introduction.

Bass have firm white flesh that can be cooked in a multitude of ways. I favor the most straightforward method of minimum implication. That is to roast sea bass whole still wearing their scales, standing in swimming position perched upon a nest of savory herbs. As described in the instruction for roasting ocean fish, the scales melt to form an outer skin, within which the succulence of the fish's flesh is held.

This method can be used to success with sea bream, gurnard, hake, whiting, butterfish, bluefish, grouper, kingfish, mullet, cod, haddock, and endless others. The key to this method of cooking is in the shape, the bodily form of the fish. If it will stand easily in swimming position and you have access to a blisteringly hot oven, this is an effective cooking method.

INGREDIENTS
—*Serves 4*

A 3 to 4 lb. (1.5kg) wild bass, or bream
Bay leaves, and savory herbs to form a nest
Extra virgin olive oil
Fleur de sel
Parsley

If the fish is without scales, or they are less pronounced—as is the case for bottom feeders, hake, and cod—simply massage the skin with olive oil, enveloping the fish in a thin layer all over. A sprinkling of fine salt administered from up high to achieve an even distribution. Execute this preparation on a clean work surface aside, with mind's eye and palate projected ahead to the pan juices. So the only salt introduced to the roasting pan is that firmly attached to the fish's oiled skin.

The bigger the bass the better the flavor will be. A bigger bite engages fuller chewing, more air in the mouth, and better olfactory stimulation. I cook fish to this method year-round; it is the accompanying vegetable, fruit, and herb garnish that evolves through the seasons. Follow the instructions for roasting ocean fish on page 174.

Once the fish is cooked, the fillets lifted and set aside wearing muslin to ward off the cold, focus on making the sauce. Full flavored as it is, you can serve sea bass with relatively neutral accompaniments. It does not require elaborate sauce. The pan juices require little reduction, nor addition of fats.

Choose a palate-cleansing herb such as parsley: chopped fine and incorporated into the juices as you work quickly, tasting as you go. Grasp the volatile floral flavor of parsley, and the moment it peaks, swiftly pass the juice through a fine sieve directly upon the fillets.

If there are few of you and the occasion is informal bring the fish to table in swimming position served upon a platter. Lift away the coat of melted scales and all help yourselves. It is a fine way for children to discover choice morsels, such as the muscle behind the head, and the fish's cheeks.

In late spring, organize accompanying dishes of new potatoes, peeled and halved, dressed in chervil and dill. Another of shelled broad beans with destoned and halved tart cherries, dressed with shoots of young basil.

Make a mayonnaise and garnish it with a dice of cherry. Lengthen to desired consistency with a small ladle of pan juices or the squeezed juice of several cherries. Serve this with an herb salad and fiercely chilled and demonstratively mineral dry white wine.

Tempura Roe

Soft herring roe is a highly nutritious and an inexpensive delicacy. Whereas most fish roe from lumpfish to caviar are the eggs of the female, soft herring roe is in fact the milt of the male fish. Japanese cuisine celebrates the milt of yellowtail, cod, salmon, and squid. They call it *shirako*, meaning the white child. Sicilians use the milt of tuna to season pasta. Russians, Scandinavians, and eastern Europeans cook the soft roe of herring.

INGREDIENTS
—*Serves 4*

21 oz. (600g) of soft herring roe
Vegetable oil

TEMPURA BATTER:
An egg yolk
10 oz. (300ml) cold water
1 ¼ cups (300g) rice flour, plus extra for dusting

TEMPURA DIPPING SAUCE:
Dashi (page 91)
Soy
Mirin
Tarragon

For the tempura batter, think in the following proportions: one egg yolk to ten parts cold water, ten parts rice flour. With chopsticks, whisk the egg yolk into the cold water and then fold in the flour in a cutting motion back and forth.

For the dipping sauce, first make a dashi. Take kombu (seaweed) and wipe it clean with damp muslin. Put this into a small saucepan and cover it generously with mineral water. Bring this to just under a boil, then take it off the heat and add a handful of dried shaved bonito flakes to taste. Stand this to infuse until the desired depth of flavor is achieved. Then strain the dashi broth through muslin. To finish the dipping sauce, add chopped tarragon, soy sauce, and mirin to taste. Herring roe, of texture similar to that of sweetbreads, calls for the same method of cooking. First stand the roe in a generous quantity of very cold water and carefully pull away any blemishes such as veins. Then in cold water, spiked with a little rice vinegar and salt, bring the soft roe to a brief and gentle simmer. This will help them hold their shape whilst they fry.

Dust the sacks of roe in rice flour. Then dip the roe into the tempura batter. Deep-fry them one by one in vegetable oil at 340°F (170°C), to crisp.

Serve with the dashi-based dipping sauce, or muslin-wrapped limes and a spiced mayonnaise might do just as well.

As garnish, you may wish to tempura some vegetables too. Depending on season use what you have to hand: a pre-summer garnish might consist of asparagus, julienned carrot, zucchini flower, and the leaves of herbs such as basil, parsley, and sage, all battered and fried to crisp in just the same way.

Sharp Eyes on the Fish Counter

Staff dinner on Fridays at Harry's Bar was a delight. Its reputation such that knife sharpeners and folk from the olive oil business would drop by the subterranean world of the kitchen perchance. The club was open from Monday to Friday. MB's logic being that the members would be in the country on the weekend. And if they weren't, well they could go to Annabel's. This meant a five-day week. Five double shifts. A rhythm representing the height of civility for kitchen types, weekends for family, perhaps even time for a life.

Ahead of the weekend on Friday afternoons, Signor Eugenio, chef garde-manger, would systemize the fish fridge. The chef entre-métiers, upon whose head fell the task of cooking staff food, would eye this up with interest. A junior chef in a brigade delegated the responsibility of feeding the staff is exposed to the judgment of all, a fast track to glory or contempt.

We always did our best to be prepared for the inevitable unexpected, to fulfill the members' whims, to satisfy the orders taken by brazen waiters ever in pursuit of tips. The headwaiter would enter the kitchen, a scribbled order waving nervously in his hand. If the expression upon his face wore a flimsy veil of smugness, masking greed, guilt, and the scent of fear, Chef would spot the demeanor just as soon as the kitchen doors swung open. "*Non mi interessa, vai su.*" Roughly translated, "I am not interested; go upstairs." Tail between his legs, the headwaiter would leave, lurk, and return, his demeanor suitably diminished and meek. Depending on Chef's mood, this ritual could in an instant escalate from jovial to cruel, leaving a waiter's ego crucified for the greater good. Banished from the kitchen to grovel servilities.

Upstairs were wealthy members and their guests, a dining room dancing to an unspoken tune of nonchalant understatement and one-upmanship.

We were well-equipped downstairs, larders full of the best ingredients anywhere in London. Harry's Bar was preceded by its reputation. And so come Friday afternoon the week's offcuts would be systemized. We'd make broths, ravioli, croquettes, and so on.

But there would still be leftovers. Cheeks of monkfish the size of sea scallops, the tails of endless huge bass, bits of belly from salmon, perhaps even tuna. Tender muscles all set aside by Signor Eugenio with his customary neatness. Dinner on Fridays was a mixed grill.

All this is to say that such treasures are to be found above ground too. Ask around and locate an especially good and busy fishmonger that provisions himself directly from independent fishermen, the sort where portly foodies routinely flock; aim to arrive late, say on Saturday after the rush. As ogres waddle off—their baskets packed with the pick of the catch—there, scattered upon the counter, left in their wake, will be

choice offcuts. Morsels not big enough to make a portion alone, and yet, these, pared into textures and colors, transcend to elegant sophistication. So keep sharp eyes fixed to the fish counter.

A cast iron griddle is the ideal piece of equipment for such cooking. Clean it thoroughly with steel wool. Then heat it and deglaze it with water until the water runs clean. The time to do this is when you have finished cooking and it is already hot. Then next time you need it, there it will be, all set.

Season the fish from up high. Always salt before oil or the seasoning will stick where it lands, in clusters. Just a sprinkling of salt and very little olive oil massaged into the fish.

Heat the griddle to high and wipe it with an olive-oil-doused branch of rosemary. The fish will cook quickly, sear it crisscross on both sides, then stand it on the vertical briefly top and tail, then let it rest. Most of the pieces you will cook would happily pass for sashimi, so take care not overcook them.

The alternative to a mixed grill is of course tempura or fritto misto. For this, use the tempura batter used for roe (page 191).

Serve a mixed grill of fish with simple accompaniments. A spiced tartar sauce might be appropriate, according to taste. Essentially a mayonnaise seasoned with a fine dice of capers and gherkins, dusted with chili, and stretched with a splash of tarragon vinegar.

Muslin-wrapped lemons immediately upgrade the situation. An herb-flower salad is probably enough. Allowing the palate to savor the many textures and flavors of the individual fish.

FUR, FLEECE, FEATHERS & HIDE

RABBIT

*

LAMB

*

CHICKEN

*

VEAL

*

BEEF

*

PORK

*

MIXED GRILL

Butchers

A litmus test to modern eating habits would show that wild meat plays little more than a walk-on part in our daily diet, with perhaps a throwaway line indulged here and there for old time's sake. Wild fish are eaten as if an infinite resource. Wild boar and deer are hunted in numbers here at Tibas. As are partridge and pretty much anything else that moves. It is all run tightly, professionally; strict seasons, quotas, syndicated and licensed hunting groups. It is due in part to the hunting of these animals that the extensive woodland that is their habitat is protected and managed with such care. Longevity is possible through nurture, not exploitation.

These wild animals live off the land, relying upon their wits, surviving on a diet of foraging; they are autonomous, enjoying freedom of movement within pockets of wilderness preserved for their benefit. So that men with guns may hunt. Fair game, and they taste good. Run around, eat what they are supposed to eat, and live freely until one unlucky day they are chased down by dogs and shot. Many domesticated animals also benefit from being reared by natural method. They too have space to run around and are fed a diet fitting to their anatomy's capacity to digest. Herbivores allowed to graze, ruminate, and graze some more, returning manure to the soil, which trodden in under hoof, feeds and composts the soil anew, to produce better pasture still. Animals destined for the table; given freedom of movement and allowed to live to maturity, whilst garnering flavor from natural diets.

The ideal is to select domesticated animals—lamb, beef, veal, pork, poultry, rabbit, and game—from butchers who are also independent farmers and stockbreeders. The next best option is to purchase meat from reputable butchers who themselves select live animals from stockbreeders. Failing that, you may find a butcher who buys traceable carcasses of butchered meat from reputable wholesalers. And failing *that*, consider skipping meat altogether. If the only available option is feedlot industrial product, ponder awhile. The day that antibiotics fail industrial scale livestock farming, the system will come crashing down, with potentially lethal viral effect for all. The happy paradox is that the finer the quality often the better the price. Buying direct from the source, free of dealers and margins, this can make economic sense. The guy you see at the farmers' market, if he can get into the city before dawn twice a week, can't live that far away.

Traceability to source has an immediate de-generalizing effect upon the understanding of the component ingredients that constitute a recipe. To have a choice of different cuts deriving from the one same animal bridges a sensorial link to the environment and the methods that have supported its production. The knowledge that the meat you eat has enjoyed a quality of life that respects its basic needs and diet, and has reached maturity before being slaughtered, instills a sense of harmony between oneself and the cyclical nature of the animal, vegetable, and mineral kingdoms. Tail and shin, rump and loin, these assume an aura of vitality. An abstracted sense of ownership over enslaved animals is replaced by an opportunity to give thanks, to celebrate the life of other living souls. A sensorial awareness that your core ingredients come from the one same animal reared by natural methods endows your cooking with respect and an aspiration to optimize the sensorial and nutritional potential of the ingredients at hand.

Rabbit

The Vernes and Monsieur Blanc keep rabbits, as do most of their peers. Between the kitchen and the vegetable garden will be a rabbit hutch where they can easily be fed on the outer leaves of vegetables and the extras from passing trugs.

Keeping rabbits is a practical application of common sense, requiring little investment beyond minimum effort and care. Rabbits breed like rabbits and provide a plentiful supply of meat. They can be fattened on leftovers, yet are vastly less implicating than keeping a pig, which demands great daily cauldrons of swill. They provide an appetizing alternative to chicken. If the hens are all laying, turning broody, and cockerels are few, it hardly seems worth wringing an egg-layer's neck. Better by far to bop a rabbit on the head and skin it for the pot.

The choice meat is to be found on the hind legs, shoulders, and saddle—the name given to the two long fillets that run up a rabbit's back. Locals here chop rabbit into stew-sized bites and it all goes into the pot with the usual garlic and parsley, potato and onion. In Tuscany they add olives and a glass of hearty wine. I find that rabbit also roasts very well. Served with a simple salad and vegetables of the kind that rabbits themselves eat.

INGREDIENTS
—*Serves 4*

A rabbit
Bay leaves
Sage
Thyme
Parsley
A teaspoon of five bays (cinq baies) peppercorn mix
A knob of butter
Extra virgin olive oil
Floral water of sage
Salt
White pepper

A little basic butchery is needed. With meat cleaver to hand, and in one clean cut, amputate the hind legs at the base of the spine just above the tail. Follow the loin to where it meets the rib cage and cut again. Leave the belly skin attached. You now have a saddle of rabbit. The deboning of shoulder and thigh is made easier with a sharpened deboning knife. Slide the scalpel-like tip of your knife down the thighbone to where it meets the knee. Whittle away and free the bone of meat on all sides. Sever the tendons that attach the bone to the knuckle. Repeat the exercise for the other thigh and both shoulders. The result: drumsticks attached to great, butterflied steaks of meat. For the saddle you will need butcher's string to truss it up. The idea is wrap it up like a parcel, one belly flap below, the other above. Garnished with herbs these serve as aromatic saddlebags.

Whilst you pre-heat the oven to 350°F (175°C), rib cage and leftover bones can be simmered in mineral water to a delicate broth that you will use to deglaze the roasting pan and make your sauce. The liver might never make it as far as table; sautéed and flambéed with brandy in the kitchen amongst cooks. Season the trussed saddle, butterflied shoulders, and thighs sparingly with salt and freshly milled white pepper. It will roast quickly in a hot oven. Garnish an iron-handled copper-based pan with a line of olive oil and a small knob of butter. As these melt, add a branch of sage, thyme, or bay to infuse; if they are freshly picked and you have abundance, add all three. There is a spice mix of different colored corns in France called five bays; it is an asset to any larder. It is composed of five types of aromatic peppercorns: black, green, white, Jamaican, and pink. Add a scattering of these to the pan and allow them to impregnate the fats. They will bring a heightened and fine mild seasoning to the finished dish.

Proceed to color the meats on all sides. Lift the bay, sage, and thyme out of the pan once they have released their flavor, and before they turn bitter. It is important to execute this stage of the cooking just so. You are branding the meats with an emotion, searing them in herb-infused fats of your design for the blistering furnace of oven to come. Keep an eye to an even coloring; arc from pink flesh to an amber glow, with no hint of burning.

Reach for new herbs and perch them upon the meats. Take a length of oven paper of sufficient size to cover the pan. Scrunch this into an ill-fitting, gap-ridden improvised lid, positioned in the manner of a hurriedly parked car. This will partly shield the crows' nest of herbs from the oven's dry heat and allow them to steam their aromas around the meat as it roasts.

Roast the meat seven minutes on each side. The belly flaps will have crisped. If they could do with a moment longer, un-truss the roast, liberate them with a knife, and return them now alone to the oven for a few minutes more. What you are looking for is texture, so that golden, and cut into thin strips, they will garnish the finished dish. Stand the thighs, shoulders, and saddle to rest awhile in a muslin-covered bowl to catch the juices.

Strain the broth that you have simmered from the rib cage and bones. Over a moderate flame, use a ladle or two of this to deglaze the roasting pan. Add the juices that have run from the resting meats, and a ladle of floral water of sage. Season these juices to taste with abundant finely chopped parsley, which will snap a gust of palate-freshening flavor to your sauce.

Again with a deboning knife, lift the loin fillets away from the bone. They are as two well-sized Cuban cigars saddled either side of the spine. With a filleting knife carve these as you would *tataki*, on the angle and to a generous gauge. Leave the shoulders and thighs just as they are. Detail a serving dish with your roast bunny, adding the thin strips of golden crisp belly. Through a fine sieve, pour over the pan juices, with a sprinkling of chopped parsley for garnish.

In late spring, you might serve this with young carrots, blanched briefly in abundant boiling water salted to a tablespoon per quart (fifteen grams per liter). Dressed with chopped tarragon, olive oil, and a shallow ladle of their cooking water. Add a side salad of dandelions for fun.

Lamb

Lamb is the name given to a sheep in its first year of life, from newborn through sexual maturity. Females that go on to breed in their second year become hoggets. Their brothers are, for the most part, slaughtered as spring lamb; those that are castrated and kept on to fatten become wethers, the meat of whom is eaten as mutton—the cleft-footed version of spur-clawed capon. Prize males are scouted and nurtured to become rams. Rams, if you are to share a space with them, require you to keep an unchallenging yet vigilantly fixed eye. Many country people walk with a limp from being cornered and charged in twilit barns by an aggressive ram. It is not to be taken personally; they are supercharged with testosterone, servicing a flock and protecting girls from rivals imagined and real.

From milk-fed lamb to mutton there is vast aperture of flavor. Sickly sweet milk-fed lamb, popular in France, Italy, and Spain, is essentially like eating babies. I see no nutritious or sensorial merit to this; it remains largely the realm of connoisseurs and ostentatious ogres. Piglets and veal are eaten in the same way and by the same ilk.

At the other end of the scale there is mutton. At its best perhaps from the carcass of a lean, eighteen-month-old castrated male—a wether—turned onto a finishing diet of spring pasture to fatten before being slaughtered in physical prime, allowing flavor to develop in muscle fat that has sprung about and lived awhile. This is the reference that we were born to at the Bailey. Homegrown meat. The prime cuts of mutton, such as a crown roast or a thick steak cut from the rump, are transcendent. Papa had a very nimble hand for butchery and never missed an opportunity to whittle away fat and size bones to elegant proportions. With butcher's string and a needle, two racks of lamb, stood upright, would be swiftly bound together to form a crown. A crown roast of mutton roasted to pink, brought forth to grace a celebratory table.

The Vernes berate the meat of today. It doesn't taste like it used to, you hear them say over and over again. Though the pigs and poultry they raise do still. And if you look a little further afield there are an increasing number of younger independent producers staying true to the principles of natural stockbreeding. Resisting the lure of scale production, they realize that once the palate acquires a reference to true flavor, it will be hard sold a pale imposter. It is possible to buy from the source. I do—be I in France or Italy or England—direct from farmers that butcher their own meat. And I am far from their only customer; these are places to meet folk with curiosity in their eyes.

Spring lamb, four to six months' old, that has been weaned and fattened on pasture is of optimum practicality. A butterflied shoulder will yield the perfect amount to feed four adults. This is a size where straightforward rapid roasting in fierce heat is an effective method of cooking.

You do not want to be wrestling great legs of mutton, charcoaled lanolin on the outside, raw in the middle. There are of course tactics to tackling larger roasts. And in time it is the honing of these skills that will allow you to enjoy huge slow roast joints of mutton. But let us focus here on a strategy of minimum implication that returns satisfaction: twenty minutes in the oven and straight to table. Shoulder is a cut of lamb marbled with fat. From the carcass of an older animal this makes for pronounced flavor. On a spring lamb the flavor is however savory sweet. It is the change in diet from milk to pasture that colors an herbivore's flesh from white ever pinker to red. Spring lamb has the color not of a rich oak-barreled Grand Cru but rather the translucent ruby glow of fine young Beaujolais. The flavor is accordingly delicate and floral. Estuary lambs are put out to graze on salt marshes to flavor their meat whilst fattening. Born in late winter and so slaughtered by June or July, be they moorland or lowland, spring lamb will have been fed and fattened on bountiful spring to summer pasture.

INGREDIENTS
—*Serves 4*

A shoulder of lamb
Rosemary
Olive oil
A knob of butter
Floral water of rosemary

GARLIC, ARTICHOKE & PARSLEY:
Four heads of new season garlic
A dozen baby violet artichokes
Abundant parsley
Fleur de sel
Olive oil
Fleur de sel
Olive oil

MASHED POTATOES:
Mashing potatoes
Bay leaves
Ginger
Chili
Olive oil
Mineral water

MINT SAUCE:
A bunch of mint
Rice vinegar
A pinch of light brown sugar

Have your butcher butterfly the blade out of the shoulder, and keep it. You will nest it back against the shoulder socket as the meat cooks to garner the flavor yielded from cooking on the bone. Yet, as the joint is spatchcocked open, the heat will penetrate its heart, enabling even roasting at a pace. Whilst you organize your weapons, pre-heat the oven to full blast 500°F (260°C). An oval double fish pan with an iron handle is the ideal roasting dish; the handle allows you to easily migrate between oven and stovetop. Remember to remind yourself to have a doubled dishcloth at hand for all maneuvers; an oven-hot handle will brand you severely across the palm of the hand. As you realize in horror what is happening, the reflex will be to grip the handle harder. Do not go there; a good fortnight of blistering pain and inconvenience looms.

Add a line of oil and small knob of butter to the pan over a moderate heat with abundant rosemary to infuse. Remember rosemary has a very volatile flavor, which in an instant will turn bitter. Infuse the pan fats guided by eye and nose.

Pepper and sparingly salt the shoulder and sear it all over, to an amber glow in the rosemary-infused fats. Bone-side down, ready the joint for the oven. A nest of rosemary perched on top, under an ill-fitting lid of scrunched cooking paper. Twenty minutes in a piping hot oven is all it takes. Pierce to the heart of the roast with a needle, and bring its tip to your lips. Warm—which means pink—is done. A bubbling spring of pink juices should emerge from where the needle pricked. To eat lamb well done defeats the object.

Remove the shoulder from the pan and stand it to rest on a serving dish, to collect the juices that run. Make your sauce in the usual way: remove excess fat, scrape the pan with a flat-headed spoon, deglaze with water or broth, add the juices that run from the resting meat, season with floral water, an aromatic herb of your choice, emulsify with olive oil, season for salt, add an abundance of finely chopped fines herbes, capture their volatile flavors, and pass the pan juices through a fine sieve and upon the carved meat. There are no rules to carving that are worth heeding. It is all pomp and prejudice. Across the grain and to the gauge you desire is enough when sending the roast straight to table. Slices cut quite thickly, for texture; a fuller bite brings more air into the mouth and triggers better olfactory stimulation. For cold cuts, reach for your prosciutto knife and sliver along the grain.

Roast lamb is an opportunity to eat mint sauce. A very British condiment, sneered at by the French. Being neither and yet both, I enjoy a mint sauce made freshly from scratch, and am bewildered by the popular commercial malt vinegar versions. To make mint sauce, proceed as for tisane: make an infusion. Use good vinegar, preferably mint-flavored rice vinegar that you have had the foresight to prepare for the larder in summer when mint is plentiful, bolts, and goes to flower. Bring vinegar up to a simmer, seasoned to taste with the bare minimum of light brown sugar. Add abundant finely chopped mint, cover with a lid, and stand it off the heat to infuse. This makes a good tart condiment to contrast and underscore the marbled fatty succulence of a shoulder of lamb.

New-season garlic, undressed of its outer skin and blanched barely a minute in salted, fiercely boiling water. Artichokes—baby violets—pared down to halves, quarters, and eighths and blanched in the garlic water. These brought together and seasoned with fleur de sel and extra virgin olive oil, garnished with abundant parsley.

To make mashed potatoes: simmer (peeled and quartered) potatoes in lightly salted water with bay leaves and chili until done. Pass them through a vegetable mill (chili and all) and then, over a lively heat with a paddle-shaped spoon, energetically beat mineral water and olive oil into the mash to the consistency you desire. Serve with an herb flower salad and a bottle of lively red wine, one too innocent by far to have ever met an oak barrel.

Chicken

Left to their own devices and natural rhythm, without interference from hormones, dark deprivation, or force-feeding, these domesticated Asian jungle fowl will reach maturity in around ninety days. It seems incredibly rapid, yet ponder: battery chicken is slaughtered from thirty days onwards. Chickens appreciate the open air; they need dust baths; they need to spread their wings, to run and mate. To peck and scratch the earth with their spur-clawed feet. A diet of assorted creepy crawlies mixed with an offering of corn suits them well. They sleep perched as high as they can. When on form, hens lay eggs daily; if they manage to hide some away, they will go broody, sitting on great nests for the twenty-one days it takes chicks to hatch. Cockerels generally ponce about, pecking order.

When possible, buy chicken with head and feet still attached. The offal should also garnish the stomach cavity—liver, gizzard, and heart—these make good private snacks for cooks, or cats. The same should be expected of quail, partridge, pigeon, woodcock, pheasant, guinea fowl, duck, and goose. Look for head, claws, and offal attached.

INGREDIENTS
—*Serves 4*

A chicken weighing 3 lbs. or less (1.5kg)
Bay leaves
Ginger
Extra virgin olive oil
Fleur de sel
Aromatic herbs of your choice, such as sage, thyme, and summer savory
Floral water of tarragon or thyme

TO GARNISH THE CARVED BIRD:
Fines herbes such as tarragon, parsley, and borage

Remove any excess fat or blood. Just as for fish, you want to thoroughly clean the stomach cavity of fowl prior to roasting to avoid any bitterness spoiling the pan juices to come. Salt the inside of the bird very sparingly, with a mind to the sauce you will make. A little salt quickly becomes irreversibly too much salt once reduced in liquid.

Massage the bird from head to foot, muscle group by muscle group. Avoid encumbering the pan with aromatic herbs, which will burn and turn bitter in the heat of the oven. Garnish the stomach cavity with bay leaves, ginger, whatever flavors you desire, but do so sparingly. If it is packed tight, full of lemon and onion and other such scrap, this will create steam and impede efficient roasting. Ask yourself which herbs and spices befit the occasion. Who are you feeding? Kids, a lover, your mother-in-law? And season accordingly.

Choose a pan neither too large (the juices would run and burn in the heat of the oven), nor too small (this would create steam and impede roasting). Again, choose a pan with an iron handle that will enable easy migration between stovetop and oven. This will serve you well when it comes to making your sauce.

Grandma Maxime's foolproof method to roasting chicken can be summarized as follows: twenty minutes three times in an oven set to 350°F (180°C). For the first twenty lay the bird on its side. Then once the timer sounds, turn the bird over onto its other thigh. For the final twenty minutes position the bird, legs and breasts in the air.

To verify that the chicken is indeed cooked, make an incision with a sharp knife to the inner thigh. If juices run clear, the bird is cooked. Turn it to rest, bum in the air, under muslin on a serving dish. All the juices will be drawn by gravity towards the breasts.

Focus now on your sauce, the usual tactics apply. With a spoon lift all excess fat from the roasting pan. Over a moderate flame and with a flat-headed spoon to hand, liberate any caramelized cooking juices from the pan's bottom. Deglaze these with water or broth. Add the juices that run from the resting meat, season with floral water, an aromatic herb of your choice, emulsify with olive oil, season for salt, add an abundance of finely chopped fines herbes, and seek to capture their volatile flavors.

An amusing way of carving a chicken is to detail it into three textures, assuring choice and plenty for all. Paper-thin breast, generous slices of deboned thigh, wings, and drumsticks. To carve the breasts paper-thin you will first need to remove the wishbone, which would otherwise hinder your knife. This is easily done. Where the neck meets the breast is where the wishbone sits; feel for it, under thumb. With the point of a knife, follow its outer contour and release it from the breast. This done, use a prosciutto knife to carve the breast. For the thighs, again under thumb, feel for the knee knuckle where drumstick meets thigh, and liberate them from one another with the tip of your knife. Debone them and roll them tight, and with a razor-sharp filleting knife, allowing the blade to do the work with the hand acting as guide, detail these to a generous gauge. Finally group together wings and drumsticks, wishbone, cardinal's nose, and oysters. Elegantly dress a serving dish with the three-textured bird; and pour the gravy directly upon it with a scattering of fines herbs.

If you have a bunch of children to feed, buy extra drumsticks and wings; roast these aside over the last blast of twenty minutes. Suddenly a chicken will feed ten. A parallel logic applies to roasting duck, pigeon, quail, and game birds; with the cooking times adjusted in accordance to size.

Just as mint and rosemary enjoy an affinity for lamb, so do tarragon and thyme for chicken. So you might finish your gravy to this effect. Thyme to infuse the juices and tarragon finely chopped to garnish the serving dish.

This is a dish you will eat year-round. The accompaniments will alter in the extreme, as the dish remains the same. Whether you are serving a summer lunch with tomato, peach, and onion salad, or an autumnal garnish of baked pears and roast chestnuts; reach to the accompanying fruit to qualify the mayonnaise you may serve alongside the bird.

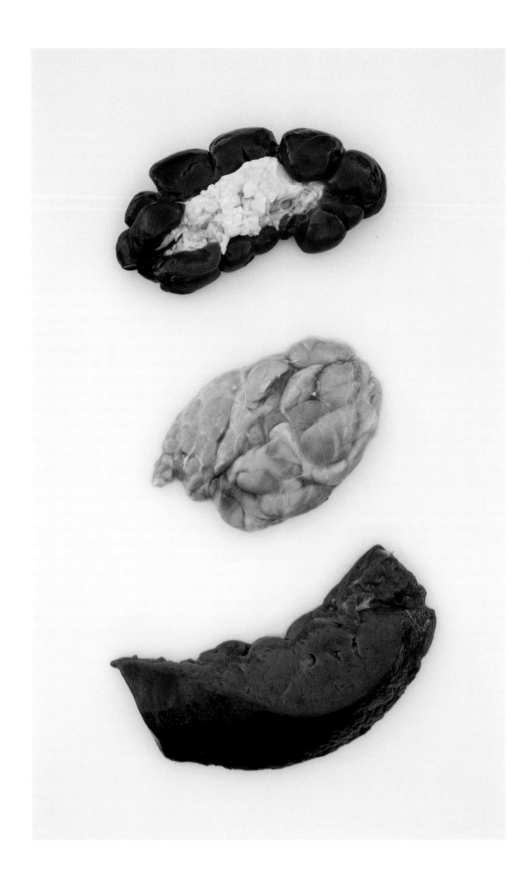

Veal

Veal is slaughtered between the ages of barely born up to eighteen months. For some, there is an emotional aversion to the idea of baby calves being separated from their mothers at birth, force-fed, and then slaughtered for the table. Many of these calves are a byproduct of the dairy industry; to lactate, dairy cows must give birth. Male dairy calves are born superfluous and are finished off in haste as value-added veal. Aversion to this practice should extend to empathy to the well being of all animals reared for slaughter: pork, poultry, dairy cows, cage-farmed fish.

In Italy there is a tradition of eating pink veal. As mentioned, the evolving color of the meat from white ever pinker to red is due to the change in diet from milk to pasture. At Harry's Bar, Chef imported pink veal from Italy and Croatia; eighteen-month-old pampered females, on the cusp of becoming beef. The markup was outrageous and demand outstripped supply.

A neighbor farms a herd of Blonde d'Aquitaine beef cattle. He uses a local slaughterhouse and does his own butchery, servicing the independent producer's market of Montauban twice weekly. He wears a well-trimmed moustache and a happy face. His wife and daughters work alongside him, the sons run the farm. The cattle are home born, given water pumped from the well, grazing fields with oaks and chestnuts for shade. In the winter the animals are fed homegrown hay harvested from spring and summer meadows. He specializes in pink veal. I travel with it for work, even to Italy.

It need not be the prime cuts, everything down to cheek and tail are of equal value and flavor. From behind his counter, he will tender a raw slice of whatever he is cutting for you to taste. Often with an anecdote: "She won second prize at show last year, presented her to the bull several times, but no joy, so she had to go. Seems a shame but . . . *tenez, monsieur, gouttez . . .*"

Offal is for Tuesdays, the day after slaughter. If you are sensitive about the provenance of meat, this is where you really want to consider what you are eating. It is the animals' liver, kidney, and sweetbreads, which will have been processing its diet. Suffice to say, the cleaner the better.

Veal liver is a super food as are kidneys and sweetbreads, the large glands of the lymphatic system that reside on either side of the heart. Hunter-gatherers would prize these the most. After felling the beast and eating its brain to possess its soul, the offal was first choice.

The pungent taste of overcooked offal is a reference held by many. However, with proper care, fresh offal cooked just so is of fine texture, delicate flavor, and highly nutritious.

INGREDIENTS
—Serves 4

14 oz. (400g) liver
14 oz. (400g) sweetbreads
A whole calf's kidney
3 bay leaves
Rosemary
A chili, cut into julienne
White pepper
Extra virgin olive oil
Fleur de sel
An onion
Parsley
A dash of rice vinegar

Start with the sweetbreads; the first step is to bathe these in icy cold water to purge them of blood and veins. Once cleaned, they should be gently blanched in simmering salted water, which will help them hold their shape for the cooking to come.

For the liver, a whole one is enough to feed an army; better by far to buy one thick slice and detail it into portions once home. First you need to clean it of the outer skin, a thin film-like covering; if you are nimble-fingered this will peel off in one go. Through the liver run veins and arteries. These require the point of a razor-sharp knife, hand-eye coordination, and patience. Follow the line of the artery and let the tip of the knife do the work. Lift them out one by one. Then detail thick steaks into half-banana-sized chunks. The texture of fresh liver cooked rare is crisp, like a bite of raw sea scallop just released from its shell. It requires seasoning, searing, and resting, no more.

Kidneys are held to the stomach wall by connective tissue and a dense fat called suet. Suet is used for savory puddings. It is pungent in flavor and wants no part of this dish. Butterfly the kidney open, and with the point of a sharp knife, patiently lift the connective suet away. A fine way of cooking kidneys is to slice them thin, season well, and sauté them over ferocious heat. Add onions and parsley, deglaze with a splash of vinegar, and that's it—Venetian style, served to garnish a saffron or rosemary risotto. In this instance, let's detail the kidney into large walnut-sized chunks.

You will need three pans, three strong stovetop burners, and the oven set to full blast. One of the joys and great divides between domestic kitchens and restaurant kitchens is that in restaurants the ovens are fired at dawn and burn till midnight. Anything started in a pan on top of the stove can be effortlessly slipped into an oven for a brief moment to cook through.

Having an ever-available heat source totally changes the way you cook. Practice for yourself with a fried egg. Put two pans onto the heat, a line of oil, and crack an egg in each. As soon as the white sets, transfer one pan to the oven for a barely a minute. As you take it out, you will see that it has evenly cooked through. A picture book fried egg. The one remaining on the stovetop, however, will be no better than the attention you have given it.

The top of the stove serves to bring ingredients up to speed; to sear a seasoned steak of calf's liver for instance, to brand it with emotion in herb infused fats of your design. The cooking, however brief, can be done in the oven. Grasp the logic; it is a dance of pans;

what have I got and what can I do with it? If the tools at your disposal are a stove with several burners and an oven, seems only common sense to turn everything on, and use it to its full potential. Visualize clearly the finished dish; be specific as to the texture, the color, the seasoning you desire, and chart the straightest path towards achieving that result.

Place the three pans over moderate heat. Garnish each with a line of oil and small knob of butter. A bay leaf cut along the spine to release its flavor, a sprig of rosemary, and a julienne of chili. Work these aromatics into the fats to infuse.

(In time you might organize for the larder a small bottle of seasoned olive oil for meats headed for grill and oven. Garnish a dark glass bottle with crushed juniper berries, rosemary, sage, and bay. Add a crushed quarter of nutmeg if you wish, and cover this with oil.)

Massage the sweetbreads, liver, and kidney with a thin covering of oil and season them with salt and white pepper. Replace the rosemary anew in all three pans. Now in with the meats; do not move them too much. Let the meats sear and color. Sparse gestures. Color one side and then the next, and then pass the pans down to the oven. The sweetbreads will take no more than a couple of minutes, followed closely by the liver, with the kidney bringing up the rear.

To finish the sweetbreads—and with a doubled dishcloth to hand—change the rosemary once more and add a little butter to the pan over a medium high flame. Once this melts, slant the pan to an angle, nose in the air. With a spoon to hand baste the sweetbreads with the rosemary-flavored fats. Then out they come, to rest upon kitchen paper under a shawl of muslin.

The liver, cooked rare, benefits from a good five minutes' resting. The kidney, cooked pink, does likewise.

Organize before you an onion sliced on a mandoline to a generous gauge that has bite, an abundance of finely chopped parsley, and some rice vinegar. Put the pans back upon the heat; remove any excess fat and distribute the sliced onion between them. Let the heat take, then as the onion begins to surrender and give up some of its liquid, start to sauté all three pans, bringing the top to the bottom, around and around.

Add parsley and sauté some more. Catch the onion before it capitulates its bite, deglazing with just enough vinegar to achieve the desired consistency—a high relish to accompany the trio of pan-roast offal. Serve with Dijon mustard, with mashed potatoes in winter; for summer, an herb-flower salad and half a white peach seasoned with olive oil and salt is probably enough.

Beef

Just as much attention to provenance is to be heeded for beef as veal, more so perhaps, as the animals are slaughtered at an older age and the window for bad diet and the administering of antibiotics and hormones is wider. Silage is nasty stuff, even the best of it harvested from organic pasture. Like alcohol, it is the product of a process of fermentation. The liver does its best to process toxins and ferret them away into body fats. Marbled rib eye of alcoholic cow anyone? So stay wide-eyed; beef, yes, but from whence?

There are breeds and bloodlines that are indigenous to regions. Despite these being undermined by standardization—the mixing of breeds for so-called size and quality, meaning speed of growth—there is a backbone of independent producers rearing herds of rare and native pure breeds. A cartoon-eye's view of cattle in popular culture will conjure a vision of black-and-white Friesians and red-hided, white-faced Herefords. This is as if the motor industry were composed solely of Ford and Volkswagen.

Friesians have been crossbred for milk yield. There are other breeds that yield milk of infinite qualities—Jersey, Guernsey, and Montbéliarde to name but three—renowned for the richness of their butter and cream. And others still that characterize the flavors of heritage cheeses that are made from the milks of specific breeds.

Longhorn, Angus, and Blonde d'Aquitaine all make fine flavored eating. Herefords have been crossbred to optimize growth and exported around the world as breeding stock. All too often they are slaughtered as beef at eighteen months, which is at least a year too early; eighteen months is more the territory of pink veal. It takes time, grazing, sheltering, and romping around for beef cattle to lay down flavor-carrying fat.

As male calves yield no milk, they are processed as veal, or expediently fattened on unnatural diets and processed as beef. Much commercial beef is the meat from such animals; lean beef—a value added by-product of the dairy industry—is correspondingly lean on integrity and flavor. Once you have scouted out a supplier or butcher that looks you in the eye when you ask him a direct question, who replies succinctly and with pride, then you have sourced beef.

Seek a butcher that can tell you the breed, the age, the provenance; detail the diet the animal was fed, how and where it was slaughtered; and in terms of flavor, explain all importantly how long the beef was hung. It is this aging process, up to three weeks in summer and five in winter, that tenderizes beef and allows it to fully develop flavor.

This is increasingly rarely done, because as meat hangs it loses moisture, and so weight. Further trimming is required when it comes to butchering the carcass down into joints. Resultantly, well-hung dry-aged beef comes with a price tag. Better to eat a shank of good beef braised in a stew than to eat a competitively priced prime cut, butchered from an unhung force-fed dairy bullock.

All the classic cuts vary slightly in name from country to country, but are more or less resumed thus: Fillet, the most expensive, most tender, and of little flavor. Sirloin, T-bone, entrecôte, rump, rib eye, top rib, topside, all make good steak. Tail, cheek, brisket, and shin make good braised stews.

Most people order a steak in accordance with the strength of their teeth: fillet for the elderly dowager, rump for her strapping grandson. Fillet, a muscle that has never worked, nestled away along the backbone, is tender and flavorless. Rump, from the buttock, having been part and party to every step the great beast has ever taken, is resultantly a muscle full of flavor, requiring sharper bite.

A thirty-month-old beef cow will weigh well over a ton. Nestled away —miniature in comparison and each weighing a kilogram or less— there are so-called "butcher's cuts": pear, spider, false spider, hampe, onglet, bavette. With these cuts, both tenderness and flavor combine. They are not expensive, though they do require making it early to market, keeping eyes peeled to the counter, and nurturing a healthy relationship with your butcher.

INGREDIENTS —Serves 4

Butcher's cuts of beef
White pepper
Fleur de sel
Extra virgin olive oil
A lime

Stand the meats at room temperature for twenty minutes or so, to optimize tenderness. Season them with salt and white pepper. Massage them with very little olive oil, and you are set. Sear them barely a couple of minutes on either side and stand them to rest. If you desire to cook them medium rare or well done, drop the pan down to the oven and cook the steak a further couple of minutes. However, at least once, try steak flash-grilled, sliced thin, and served with olive oil, fleur de sel, and a squeeze of lime. Dare to equip yourself with the sensorial reference of rare steak; you may never look back.

To test whether meat is done there is a slightly silly but effective trick. With your index finger apply pressure to the cooked surface of the meat. The texture of lips is rare; of the chin, medium rare; and the tip of the nose, well done.

A rocket salad dusted with chili and seasoned with horseradish vinegar and salt is sufficient accompaniment. Lay the table with extra virgin olive oil, fleur de sel, and muslin-wrapped lime. You may add mustard for those that wish, a horseradish sauce perhaps, although both of these condiments are more the realm of a roast joint of beef. Here, the point is to savor the fine texture and flavor of butcher cuts.

Pork

A slow roast belly of pork. A salted ham simmered with onion, mace, and cloves, and served with parsley sauce. Loin chops, rump steaks, a whole roast rack of pork cutlets brought to the table and carved. A filet mignon for the elderly dowager, skin scored into strips and crisped to crackling grissini to dip in spiced applesauce. A rolled and truffle-stuffed trotter to eat with lentils on New Year's Day. *"Tout est bon dans un cochon"*—the Vernes certainly think so. Every last scrap is used, salted and cured, the carcass scraped, fat rendered, intestine used to house sausage and salami. Everything—down to the blood that pumped around the deceased beast's veins—is knowingly processed and at some point over the next year brought forth to table. Be ruthless as to where you source pork; be under no illusion as to the vileness of the pork industry.

My favorite cut is the chine. It is a fat-marbled joint, lifted from where the shoulder meets the loin. The equivalent cut from beef is referred to as rib eye. You can cut these into steaks and grill them over charcoal, or start them off in a pan followed by the now habitual migration south for a quick blast of oven. In winter a joint of roast chine and its crackling are a joy. Roast pink and carved paper-thin. Served with cabbage, roast onions, orchard fruit en papillote, and a peppery rocket salad. To eat pork pink is deemed madness. We are conditioned against it. And in no way do I encourage you to test this for yourself. Yet in every butcher shop or farmer's barn where I have been privy to the preparing of salami, I have seen and indeed partaken in the tasting and seasoning of raw pork meat. Checking salami for seasoning incurs tasting the mix. Leaner meats and carcass scrapings ground together to a fatter or finer gauge, and salted and peppered to taste. In Tuscany, early in the week following the slaughter day that is Monday, a typical farmer's winter breakfast is composed of a slice of bread grilled over the fire, with highly seasoned raw pure pork sausage spread upon it. New season olive oil and parsley, an espresso corrected with grappa, *e avanti*.

INGREDIENTS
—*Serves 4*

A 4 to 5 lb. (2kg) chine roast of pork with skin attached
Extra skin for crackling (if desired)
Bay leaves
A knuckle of ginger
A stalk of lemongrass
Fennel seeds
Mace
An onion
An apple
A quince
Apple juice
Sage floral water
Sage or other aromatic herb
Olive oil
Fleur de sel
Fines herbes

FRUIT GARNISH:

A pear
A quince
An onion
Bay leaves
A knuckle of ginger
Star aniseed
A chili

FOR THE APPLESAUCE:

4 tart apples
Bay leaves
Ginger
Apple juice, or mineral water

Ask your butcher for a chine roast with the skin left attached. If he looks at you blankly, having already jointed the roast free of its skin, ask him for a corresponding length, say from the loin. A cut such as chine is housed within thick-skinned fat.

The objective is to transform the skin into crisp crackling and gently roast the meat to the optimum point of doneness. If the temperature of the oven is too high, the succulence of the meat will be compromised, although the crackling might be a resounding success. The answer lies in a little knife work. Remove the skin in one piece, score it and then re-garnish the joint with the skin trussed upon it, ready for the oven. You might remove excess fat from the joint whilst doing so, and season the meat within. Fennel seeds, bay leaves, grated fresh ginger, or mace. Once the meat is cooked, return the scored skin to the oven, to crisp.

With the sharp tip of a filleting knife work your way under the skin, cut along the edge with steady hand; continue to peel it back cutting around the joint, lifting up the skin in one piece. To score it, a box cutter is most effective. Score long thin strips to within a thumb's breadth of the edges, so that by the time you have finished, the skin is detailed like the grill of a racing car.

Pre-heat the oven to 350°F (175°C). Roughly chop an onion, an apple, and a quince. Detail the roasting tray with these. They will prevent the joint from drying as it roasts and form the building blocks of the pan juices to come. Add knuckles of ginger, bay leaves, and lemongrass if you have it to hand. Place the chine upon this aromatic bed and into the oven; cover with an ill-fitting oven-paper scrunched lid. It will take a good two hours. Keep an eye on progress. If the pan looks dry, add a ladle or two of apple juice. The aromatics want a damp meadow-like environment, not a desert plain.

After ninety minutes remove the oven-paper lid and prick the joint to the heart with a pin. If all is well, the juices will run pink and furiously. If you have a meat probe thermometer this is a good time to check on progress. The optimum final heart temperature is 145°F (63°C). Take stock of how far from attaining this temperature you are. Discard the herbs and return the pan to the oven, all whilst monitoring the heart temperature, as it progresses to done. Once achieved, stand the joint covered with muslin on a serving dish to rest. Garnish a roasting dish with a pastry grill, to receive the un-trussed skin. The grill will allow drainage of excess fat and prevent burning. Return the scored skin to the oven to crackle. Keep an eye on it.

During this time you will have industriously taken advantage of the lit oven. Pears and quince, peeled, cored, halved, and quartered, and wrapped up into parcels of greaseproof paper with bay leaves and shavings of ginger. These will steam bake in the oven to become your savory fruit garnish. To the same method, prepare onions: undressed of their peel and the first layer or two of coarser skin, then halved, taking care to leave them attached at the root, thus holding form. Add star aniseed and chili for company. Place each parcel upon a roasting tray in the oven. They will accompany the pork over the final half hour or so of cooking.

Depending on quality, you might roast whole heads of garlic just as they are, standing to attention in a little pan. Twenty minutes should do, until they just surrender to touch. If they burn throw them away or they'll ruin the lunch. The roast garlic squeezed from the cloves, then seasoned with olive oil, finely chopped parsley and salt makes a condiment. If you can find spring cabbage, buy it; if you can find the seed, grow it. It is conical in shape and the finest in flavor of all the cabbages. Cut it along the vertical, and then into finger width strips. Wash it under cold water, checking for errant slugs. And then throw it into a pan over high heat, still wet with the residual water of its rinsing. Add olive oil, a little butter, fleur de sel, and a twist of black pepper. Close the lid. It will take barely a couple of minutes over a fierce flame.

Pork has a natural affinity for apples, so rustle up a bay and ginger-spiced applesauce to celebrate this synergy. Peel the apples, then halve, quarter, and core them. Chop them finely and put them straight into a pan with a coarse knuckle of ginger and bay leaves. Add a ladleful of mineral water or apple juice and turn up the heat to full blast. Once the pan hits the boil, turn the flame right down as far as it will go and close the pan with a lid. Keep an eye on it and taste regularly; with the lid closed the sauce cannot reduce, which allows the aromatics to do their work. Once you are satisfied with the flavor, remove the lid and reduce the sauce to desired consistency. Pass it through a vegetable mill, and that's it.

Having allowed the chine a good fifteen minutes to rest, now carve it with a prosciutto knife into paper-thin slivers that you might detail into petals circling a large serving dish. You will have also remembered to keep a sharp eye on the crackling, which by now will be crisp. To make the sauce, the habitual logic applies. Remove excess fat, scrape the pan with a flat-headed spoon; in this instance there is a wealth of residue thanks to the onion, apple, and quince. Deglaze the pan with water or broth; add the juices that run from the resting meat, season with floral water (sage), an aromatic herb of your choice (sage again). Emulsify with olive oil, season for salt, add finely chopped fines herbes, and seek to capture their volatile flavors. Pass the pan juices through a fine sieve and directly upon the carved meat.

Serve to table the steam-baked apple and quince dressed in new season olive oil and salt, the spicy winter rocket salad dressed with dill vinegar, the paper-thin petals of chine, ginger spiced applesauce, and abundant crisp crackling.

Mixed Grill

A mixed grill is decidedly best enjoyed in a rustic setting with rustic ingredients. Grilled over the hearth in winter, on a Sunday with friends and wine over lunch. Everybody partaking in the task: lighting the fire, bringing in the wood, opening bottles, kids passing around salami and cheese as you cook. Grownups washing salads and picking herbs. Such a meal brings a kitchen to life. Folk focused on fire, together convivial, in a team effort to land lunch.

Shop for a minimum of three cuts. If you buy, say, a leg of lamb and cut it into cigarette-packet-sized steaks, this is good. The chine we have just roasted could be detailed into cuts of equal-sized thickness. Great lengths of pure pork sausage are super simple and will shut up the kids. And perhaps, as a star piece—eyes will clock it from the moment it is unwrapped—a great thick forerib of beef or veal, to grill steadily to rare on the bone.

These, carved and brought to table, elegantly displayed on one huge platter; served with bitter winter salads and dishes of beans dressed in new season olive oil, raw onion, and parsley; this is timeless and high-rustic eating.

A simple accompaniment might perhaps be white beans: coco blancs, or borlotti. Fresh in the summer shucked from their pods. Covered with mineral water and brought to the brink of a simmer, air bubbles barely rising through the water, cooked thus for the twenty minutes or so until done. To the cooking broth add aromatics and a slug of olive oil to encourage a loose emulsion to form and carry these flavors into the broth.

In winter, use dried beans. Soak these overnight in abundant cold water, changing the water when you have occasion to. Then proceed as above.

Once they are just cooked, transfer them to a cold receptacle to halt cooking and allow them to cool in their broth. Finely dice an onion, taking care not to bruise it as you proceed. Organize a fine dice of tender parsley stalks—so fine they are almost invisible—again taking care not to bruise them in order to nurture their texture. Diced stalks of peppery rocket work well too.

Place the diced onion and parsley into a saucepan and add the beans. Cover them barely up to their waists in cooking broth, and then gently bring the pan up to warm.

Then off the heat, season the beans and their shallow broth with new season extra virgin olive oil to taste. Add parsley, season for salt, a pinch of the grated rind of a lemon perhaps, and that's it.

Serve young light wine, *vin qui se boit tout seul* ("wine that drinks itself"). Half of the point of this menu is the communion it invites.

ICES

BLOOD ORANGE SORBET

✻

APPLE SORBET

✻

RHUBARB SORBET

✻

COFFEE GRANITA

✻

TANGERINE GRANITA

✻

MOONSHINE, BOOZE & LIQUEUR GRANITE

✻

BITTER CHOCOLATE ICE CREAM

✻

VANILLA ICE CREAM

✻

HONEY ICE CREAM

✻

STRAWBERRY FROZEN YOGURT

Sorbet

The craft of pastry calls for a more scientific sensibility than the savory kitchen. I was trained under Signor Aldo at Harry's Bar. Aldo is very precise, as pastry chefs often are. He trained at the Savoy in the 1950s, when it still had the original kitchen layout designed by Escoffier. He worked methodically from seven a.m. to seven p.m., day in day out. His apprentice oversaw the dinner service, and as fate would have it, at one time, that was me.

Iced sorbets and *granite* can be made from fruit juices, purees, booze, cordials, and flavored waters such as tisanes and coffee. They provide a refreshing and palate-cleansing way to end a meal—as long as they are not riddled with hidden sugar. Nero apparently served his guests a mixture of crushed fruit with mountain snow and honey, which sounds worth trying. Though it might be easier to take fruit and honey to the mountain than to bring snow to Rome.

I do not have a sweet tooth, so the challenge with Aldo in the pastry kitchen was always how to add less sugar. I started by secretly diluting the syrup in the fruit salad with the juice wrung out of a mango pip or other such succulent compost. When it came to sorbets, early on, I'd try to discreetly increase the ratio of fruit juice to syrup.

Neutral stock syrup, as it is referred to in a pastry kitchen, is made by bringing equal parts sugar and water to the boil, so as the sugar dissolves, the two become one. If the temperature is taken much higher to 237°F (114°C) you will obtain so-called invert sugar. This vile-sounding but harmless concoction is useful for making frozen yogurt. Syrup is a blank canvas that can then be qualified with the taste of the fruit to be iced. The juice of the fruit gives the mixture its flavor. So for apple, rhubarb, mint, or other infusions, you aim to season the chosen juice sprightly. Add a squeeze of lemon to a juice too sweet, a pinch of sugar to one too tart, and so forth.

With a citrus sorbet one has another weapon. The taste of a blood orange, for instance, will be carried into a sorbet by infusing the syrup with the fruit's zest. What remains to be done is to combine the desired proportion of the infused syrup to the freshly squeezed juice, then churn the mixture. I would discreetly concoct and season Aldo's sorbet mix to my palate. A subtle and clean taste provided by the zest-infused syrup, balanced with the palate-stimulating flavor of juice.

This is where it gets trickier, for the texture of sorbet is determined by several factors. Firstly and most importantly, the proportions of the added ingredients: it is sugar—the syrup—that gives longevity of elasticity to the ice. Then there is the means by which the sorbet is churned, which is to say, the efficiency of the machine used. And finally, the temperature at which you choose to serve the sorbet. It is worth noting that to achieve optimum texture, a service freezer for ices should be set at the illegally high temperature of 17°F (-8°C). And in restaurants they usually are.

At Harry's Bar we used the Rolls Royce of sorbet machines, a Carpigiani from Italy. Such a machine freezes and churns incredibly efficiently. Rapid temperature reduction harnessed with strident churning incorporates air into the mix, resulting in a pleasing light, fluffy texture. The key is to watch it like a hawk, and catch it the moment it is done.

When facing a domestic sorbet machine the trick is to chill the syrup and juice mixture in the freezer for twenty minutes. That way the machine need not waste energy chilling the mix, and can focus on the task of churning.

As it churns, water in the sorbet mixture will freeze into tiny crystals of ice. The higher the proportion of syrup in the mixture, the tighter these crystals are bound together and the smoother the texture of the ice will be, and vice versa. The longer the sorbet is kept, the more this is apparent.

With this in mind, most commercial sorbets are riddled with glucose syrup and inverted sugar to give them pseudo-infinite shelf life. My heart always goes out to folk who think they are eating "light" by ordering sorbet. Oftentimes one is better off having ice cream or frozen yogurt, where the higher fat content cooperates with the pastry chef to achieve unctuous texture with less sugar. Most sorbets contain at least twice the sugar of ice cream.

This is why Aldo would rumble me. For my sorbet—despite having the desired texture and tasting heavenly as it cascaded from the Carpigiani, and for several hours thereafter— would, due to the reduced proportion of sugar in the mixture, find itself by the next day solid as a rock, and crystallized.

Having understood this, and, standing dutifully ashamed, I respectfully apologized and kept the logic under my hat, awaiting the day I had a pastry kitchen under my own jurisdiction.

The answer is: if a sorbet with little sugar has a reduced shelf life, then make it to order. Up the street at George we would churn sorbets twice a day before each service. It is common sense, especially in a domestic context, where making sorbet is not an everyday occurrence. So when you do make it, why not prepare and chill the ingredients in advance, then churn it as you are cooking dinner so as to serve your guests clean stimulating sorbet, full of vitality.

Granita

A granita is less unforgiving than a sorbet. Whereas a sorbet is judged as much by its unctuous texture as it is by flavor, a granita, is by definition, a serving of flavored ice crystals.

Even if disaster strikes—the phone rings or premature dementia kicks in, and the whole mix turns rock solid—you can scrape it and chop it and elbow grease it into shape. Lazy assistant pastry chefs in fact do precisely this. They freeze it solid and chop it with a knife. Then you fire them.

Assemble your chosen concoction of fruit juice, booze, flavored waters, infusions, cordials, and corresponding syrups. Then combine juice and syrup to taste. Place the mixture in a wide, shallow, stainless steel dish in the freezer. Every quarter of an hour or so, with a whisk to hand, break up the forming ice crystals, working the faster freezing edges to the center to homogenize the mix. Continue to whisk at intervals over the course of several hours until the mixture has frozen into a dust of jewel-like crystals.

A quenelle of sorbet in a frozen glass garnished top and bottom with a scattering of granita is a way of transforming clean ingredients into an elegant dessert. Seek, with palate and eye, to compose pairings that enhance one another.

Ice Cream

Ice cream should in fact be called iced cream, sugar, milk, eggs, and flavorings. It is essentially aromatic, sweet frozen custard. As with all endeavors in the pastry kitchen, the first step is to scrupulously weigh out all of the ingredients. Line them up before you, complete a pre-flight checklist of tools, clear the path ahead, and commence.

In brief, the task list reads: simmer milk and some of the sugar. Whisk egg yolks and remaining sugar together with this simmered sweet milk. Return the resulting proto-custard to the heat, and cook it *à la nappe*. Take it off the heat, add flavorings to infuse; chill the mixture in an iced bain-marie. Pass the mixture through a fine sieve. Add cream and churn. Now with a bit more detail: First place the egg yolks with one third of the sugar into a generous-sized bowl. Bring the remaining two thirds of sugar up to a simmer in the milk, whisking to combine, so that the sugar melts and the sweetened milk becomes one homogeneous mass. Do not let it boil or the flavor will be irreversibly spoiled.

Once this is done, make your crème anglaise, or custard base. Beat the egg yolks and sugar together stridently. Gently pour the sweetened milk upon the sugar-blanched egg yolks, all whilst whisking to combine. Start slowly, and then as the mixture amalgamates and becomes one, pour in the rest of the milk in a steady flow, whisking as you go.

Transfer this custard base to a clean saucepan and put it upon a moderate flame. Whisk constantly in a gentle circular motion, bringing the edges of the pan to the center. Have a spatula at hand. The objective is to cook the mixture *à la nappe*. This is determined by dipping the tongue of the spatula into the custard, holding it horizontally, and running your finger across the sauce coating it. The moment the line retains its straight edge (that is, the sauce does not immediately run over it) it is cooked *à la nappe*. Immediately take the pan off the heat. A moment too long will result in scrambled eggs.

Add flavoring specific to your recipe, say, honey or finely grated bitter chocolate, and stand to infuse. When the desired depth of flavor is attained, transfer the ice cream base to a clean bowl and set it in an iced bain-marie. Once the temperature has cooled to a refrigerator-friendly level, base can be kept in the refrigerator overnight, so that the flavors may infuse further. To finish the ice cream, pass the mixture through a fine sieve, pushing it through with the back of a small ladle, before adding chilled double cream. Whisk the mixture stridently to become one homogeneous mass. Set your ice cream machine to its chilling setting. Add the prepared base and, with an eye as sharp as a hawk, churn ice cream to the desired consistency.

Remember to serve ices in frozen, heavy-bottomed glasses. A frozen whisky tumbler does the trick. Guests can then continue to enjoy conversation and the transition from wine to eaux de vie, all whilst the iced dessert politely awaits judgment.

Blood Orange Sorbet

The taste of a citrus fruit that hits the tongue emanates from the zest, the flavor that you pick up with the nose from its juice. Both sweet and bitter oranges are native to China and are hybrids of the pomelo and the mandarin.

The blood orange is a mutation of the sweet orange and it benefits from both pronounced flavor and fragrant zest. Blood orange season bridges late autumn through winter and into early spring. If mandarins are in season, so are blood oranges. Their vivid color comes from anthocyanin pigments that develop when exposed to just the right balance of cold nighttime temperatures and warm sunny days.

The Sicilian autumn and winter climate offer the perfect conditions, and the Arancia Rossa produced there is particularly fine. It enjoys protected geographical status (PDO) like Parmesan, Roquefort, and Champagne, and makes a highly satisfactory sorbet that is vibrant in color, and faintly tart and sweet to palate.

INGREDIENTS
—*Serves 6*

18 oz. (550ml) freshly squeezed blood orange juice

FOR THE SYRUP:
¾ cup (150g) castor sugar
3½ oz. (100ml) mineral water
Pith-free blood orange zest

With a vegetable peeler and a gentle turn of hand, meticulously peel the zest away from several blood oranges in strips. If there is any bitter pith (the inner white part of the rind) remaining, take a sharp filleting knife and lift it away. The amount of zest you use to flavor your syrup is entirely up to you, and one might argue that there can never be too much. But be sure that it is free of pith or else the sorbet will be ruined.

Measure out the sugar and the mineral water, and add the zest. Bring these up to a boil over a fierce flame. Once the syrup hits the boil and has become one homogeneous mass, stand it to infuse whilst you juice the oranges.

You need 18 oz. (550ml) of juice. Here again, whether you use an electric citrus juicer or a more basic tool, proceed with gentle hand. You do not want to grind the pith into the juice. Filter the juice through a fine sieve to eliminate errant pips and fiber.

Once you are satisfied with the depth of taste that the zest has imparted to the syrup, you may strain it into a clean bowl, and place it upon a nest of ice to chill. You will reduce the temperature even quicker with the help of a whisk.

This done, combine the juice and the syrup and place the mixture in the freezer for twenty minutes before churning it in your sorbet machine.

Serve in frozen tumblers. For grownups you might want to scatter a dusting of coffee granita on top, or perhaps even coffee granita that has been "corrected" with grappa.

Cox & Bramley Apple Sorbet

The ancestor of the apple we know today originated in the Tian Shan Mountains nestled between the unwelcoming Gobi Desert and the Mongolian plain. These wild fruit forests, high in the mountains of Central Asia, were nurtured by the warm winds of the Indian Ocean to the south and relatively protected from the outside world. Apart from travelers and traders braving the perilous mountain passes, this area has enabled fruit trees to evolve peacefully for millennia.

The tastier specimens of these wild apples were eaten, *scrumped* by man and beast as they passed through, and the seeds from these fruit cast ever further westward along the trade routes, where some would germinate, drop root, grow and hybridize with related species. Some of these wild apples are delicious, yet, much as the crab apple, a lot of them—although suitable for cider, applejack, and animal fodder—are too bitter to palate.

The Chinese discovery of grafting permitted the domestication of the trees with better-tasting fruit. (Grafting is the process of healing a branch of wood from a desirable tree into a hardy rootstock. The grafted tree grows and bears fruit characteristic of the introduced variety.) The Etruscans and Romans further refined this technique and introduced the ancestors of contemporary varieties we know ever further westward.

Monasteries provided safe havens for domesticated apple varieties through the Dark Ages, and today their guardianship inspires a cohort of orchard farmers who strive to conserve and market these inherited and diverse varieties.

In the northern hemisphere, depending upon variety and altitude, apples are harvested from mid-August through early October. If they are then stored in a temperature- and humidity-controlled environment, apples will stay crisp from August until March. Apple juice bottled at harvest time can obviously be enjoyed throughout the year.

Commercially grown apples figure among the most pesticide-laden of fruit, so wherever possible, source your apple juice direct from a producer who farms by natural method. Keep an eye out for variety-specific unfiltered pure apple juice that has been pressed and bottled at harvest, when apples are at their very best. And keep in mind that there are many farmers working by natural methods who for various reasons choose not to register their agriculture as organic. Just as there is an ever-increasing amount of organic-labeled produce hitting the shelves that outsources labor and production to far-flung sites with hidden environmental and human costs.

A multitude of apple varieties exist, each offering variances in texture and flavor. For sorbet, which will need to have sugar in the form of syrup added, I suggest using the juice of a tart apple. Many producers press Bramley cooking apples and Cox eating apples together into a lively blend.

INGREDIENTS — *Serves 6*

18oz. (550ml) apple juice
¾ cup (150g) castor sugar
3 ½ oz. (100ml) mineral water
½ tsp. (2.5g) pectin powder
Lemon juice, to taste

Make stock syrup with the water and sugar. Stir in the pectin powder to dissolve. Allow syrup to cool and then strain it through a fine sieve into a bowl. Combine with the apple juice. Season this mixture to taste with a squeeze of lemon. Chill the mixture in the freezer for a quarter of an hour, and then churn in a sorbet machine.

Watch it like a hawk and rescue the sorbet from the machine the moment its texture cascades into one unctuous mass. An hour in the deep freezer will improve texture and flavor.

Rhubarb Sorbet

There is contention in some quarters as to whether rhubarb is a vegetable or a fruit. It was classified as a fruit by a U.S. court in the early twentieth century, but this probably had as much to do with trade tariffs as botany. Rhubarb pushes up through the soil in mid to late spring, and though it is essentially a vegetable, folk in the Northern hemisphere optimistically embrace it as a fruit.

There are different methods to processing rhubarb for sorbet. Some stew it with sugar and a little water, although this compromises the color. In fact rhubarb only really became popular in the West as sugar became more affordable. When making sorbet, I prefer to use a centrifugal juicer, which dispenses with the fibrous stalks, leaving you with just the tart pink juice. A rhubarb sorbet is eye-catching, the perfect Yves Saint Laurent pink.

INGREDIENTS — *Serves 6*

17 oz. (500ml) rhubarb juice
¾ cup (200ml) stock syrup

For rhubarb, use plain stock syrup—and whatever you do, do not infuse it with the leaves. Eating the leaves will do you no good; if you eat a barrow-load they will kill you. They contain poisonous toxic compounds.

Thoroughly wash the rhubarb stalks, cutting away the great elephant-eared leaves a good half-inch from the stem. And then this is a recipe so simple it almost makes itself: juice the rhubarb, combine it with the neutral stock syrup, chill the mixture, and then churn it.

Serve in a frozen tumbler. This makes for an eye-catching and effective palate cleanser following hearty dishes.

Coffee Granita

The appeal of this granita hangs upon the quality of its component ingredients. Think along the lines of fine espresso and naturally produced chemical-free grappa, or moonshine of any variety. You will have perhaps witnessed in Italy the topping up of an espresso with moonshine—"correcting it" is the vernacular.

The following proportions easily fill half a dozen tumblers. Or if you are using the granita as a garnish, for a tangerine or blood orange sorbet for instance, this amount will go much further.

INGREDIENTS
—*Serves 6*

13 oz. (375ml) coffee
½ cup (95g) granulated sugar
Grappa
Alternatively for teetotalers, floral water of rose, to taste

Make the coffee, cup by cup, percolator by percolator. There is no point in doing this with filter coffee; it simply will not make the cut.

Whisk the sugar into the coffee whilst it is still hot. The amount given in the ingredients list is geared to my palate. If you prefer it sweeter go ahead—there are no rules.

If you want plain coffee granita, simply pass the sweetened coffee mixture through a fine sieve and directly into a shallow stainless steel dish. Place it in the deep freezer and whisk.

Alternatively, rose water can be a good addition, which adds another dimension of flavor. In general, a splash of rose water in a cup of coffee is highly preferable to sugar. But what we really want to add is grappa. As we shall see in the next recipe, when making ices with alcohol, the key is the proportion of water to liquor. Since our sweetened coffee is flavored water and syrup in one, here we just need to add grappa, making it stronger or weaker according to taste.

Pass the coffee and grappa mixture through a fine sieve and directly into a shallow stainless steel dish, and place it in the deep freezer. Proceed with the freezing and whisking process and continue for as long as it takes. If covered airtight in the freezer, a granita will keep for a good couple of weeks. Some flavors may even improve.

Tangerine Granita

Tangerines, mandarins, and seedless clementines have a lot going for them. They are smaller, sweeter, better flavored, and easier to peel than oranges. You can slip a couple in your pocket and eat them on the go. Children excitedly retrieve them from their Christmas stockings, which can be useful indeed: a child with a fever will happily eat vitamin C–spiked tangerine granita.

INGREDIENTS
—*Serves 6*

18 oz. (550ml) of freshly squeezed tangerine juice

FOR THE SYRUP:
¾ cup (150g) of castor sugar
5 oz. (150ml) of mineral water
Pith free tangerine zest

Here again the rule for citrus fruit applies: remember the taste is in the zest and the flavor in the freshly squeezed juice. With a sharp vegetable peeler carefully lift strips of zest off the tangerine. Remove any remaining pith with the sharp flexible blade of a filleting knife.

Measure out the water, and add the castor sugar, and zest. Bring this up to a boil over a fierce flame, whisking until the sugar dissolves. Once it has hit the boil and has become one homogeneous mass, stand it to infuse away from the stove whilst you juice the tangerines.

Whether you use an electric citrus juicer or a more basic tool, proceed with gentle hand. You do not want to grind the pith into the juice. Filter the juice through a fine sieve to eliminate errant pips and fiber.

Once you are satisfied with the depth of taste that the zest has imparted to the syrup, you may strain it into a clean bowl, and place it upon a nest of ice to chill. You will reduce the temperature even quicker with the help of a whisk.

Combine the juice and chilled syrup and pour it directly into a shallow stainless-steel dish, and place it in the deep freezer. Proceed as usual. With a whisk in hand, break up the forming of ice crystals, working the faster freezing edges into the center to homogenize the mix. Continue to whisk at intervals over the course of several hours until the mixture has frozen into a dust of jewel-like crystals.

Moonshine, Booze & Liqueur Granite

You probably keep vodka and moonshine in the freezer and are all too aware that hard liquor does not freeze. The trick to making granite from such firewater is simply to dilute the booze with sparkling water and stock syrup.

For a successful result, the proportion of each should be one part moonshine—45% alcohol by volume (ABV)—four parts stock syrup, and five parts sparkling water.

100ml grappa
12 oz. (400ml) stock syrup
17 oz. (500ml) sparkling water

You can up the proportion of booze to syrup inversely with the proof of alcohol. So for instance, if using a liqueur of around 20% ABV you can double the booze and reduce the syrup:

200ml liqueur
6 oz. (200ml) stock syrup
17 oz. (500ml) sparkling water

For champagne (around 12% ABV), you can more than double the booze again, leaving just enough for a handsome glass from a regular 750ml bottle.

600ml champagne
6 oz. (200ml) stock syrup
7 oz. (200ml) sparkling water

Pass the mixture through a fine sieve and directly into a shallow stainless steel dish, and place it in the deep freezer. Every quarter of an hour or so, with a whisk to hand, break up the forming ice crystals, working the faster freezing edges into the center to homogenize the mix. Continue for as long as it takes, whisking at intervals over the course of several hours until the mixture has frozen into a dust of jewel-like crystals.

Bitter Chocolate Ice Cream

Theobroma cacao—food of the gods—is the Latin name given to the tree that bears the fruit from which chocolate derives. The transformation of these fruits into chocolate requires a three-stage process: fermentation, roasting, and grinding.

Indigenous to Central America, the cacao tree yields large seed-carrying pods, which once harvested are broken open and put to ferment. The degree of care that is taken to do this determines the quality of flavor of the chocolate to come. After fermentation, the beans are dried and then roasted to develop flavor. These roasted cacao beans are ground into chocolate liquor that is then separated into cacao butter and cacao solids (which if ground further yield cacao powder). The combination of these two ingredients, to varying proportions, gives us basic unsweetened chocolate that is 100% cacao. The percent listed on a bar of chocolate refers to the proportion of cacao to sugar in the finished product. So-called sweet chocolate has sugar added; milk chocolate has milk added in one form or another; and white chocolate contains sugar and milk, but no cacao solids.

The ancient Central American way to consume chocolate was as an invigorating brew of chocolate liquor diluted with water or other liquids and seasoned with chili, honey, or spices. This was the manner in which chocolate was consumed in Europe for centuries: a hot drink sweetened with sugar, milk, cream, and later, vanilla.

Bitter chocolate, that is to say chocolate containing 60% or more cacao liquor, makes fine ice cream. The flavor of chocolate is complex and to my palate diminished by the addition of excessive sugar. If you aspire to an aftertaste worthy of the gods, the chocolate used must be bitter enough to withstand the pastry chef's onslaught of cream, milk, eggs, and sugar.

INGREDIENTS
—Serves 6

15 oz. (425g) chocolate, 61% cacao, extra bitter
6 egg yolks
1 cup (240g) sugar
24 oz. (700ml) milk
13 oz. (375ml) double cream

Proceed as follows, referring to the introductory notes on ice cream (page 230) where and as needed for more detailed instruction.

Simmer milk and some of the sugar. Whisk egg yolks and remaining sugar together with this simmered sweet milk. Return the resulting proto-custard to the heat, and cook it *à la nappe*. Take it off the heat; add finely grated bitter chocolate to melt, whisking to combine. Chill the mixture in an iced bain-marie. Pass the mixture through a fine sieve to remove all lumps. Add cream and churn.

Honey
Ice Cream

Prior to the large-scale production of sugarcane and the current stranglehold that sugar has on the contemporary diet, honey was the only conservable sweetener available in a pure and natural state, apart from perhaps the flesh of certain dried fruit.

Bees produce honey as a food source—it is what they eat (their insurance policy against the depths of winter). Relocating swarms of bees into man-made hives has allowed us to semi-domesticate them and harvest their honey.

The multi-billion-dollar global commercial food industry depends upon the European honeybee, *Apis mellifera*, as the pollinators of crops and plants. Without the tireless work of the honeybee, food production would collapse.

When a bee visits a flower to collect nectar, it brushes against pollen held on the stamens, the flower's male reproductive organs. The bee, still carrying this pollen, upon entering the next flower it visits, may rub itself on the stigma, or female productive organ. This cross-pollinates and fertilizes the flower, which will now produce fruit. To pollinate is to fertilize, and thus enable the growth of plants, vegetables, and fruit.

Monoculture and heavy use of pesticide has decimated populations of wild pollinators over the course of the last century. Nowadays pollination depends upon the seasonal shuttling of honeybees back and forth across countries and continents to keep the ecosystem in order. They start their season fertilizing orchards in the south, then the hives are packed onto trucks and shuttled ever further north throughout the flowering season. This is big business and precarious, as bees are not to be taken for granted. Alarming numbers of bees are mysteriously dying at a scale of colony collapse. It seems to be directly linked to changes in agricultural methods, and the employment of ever more sophisticated and lethal pesticides.

The wonder of honey, or honeys, is that there is such diversity of flavor. Each flower has its distinct fragrance and perfume. From the lightest and most delicate springtime essences to the strong sun-kissed flavors of high summer.

Hives are harvested twice a year: at mid-summer once the flowering meadows have been cut for hay, which yields so-called spring flower honey, and then again at summer's end.

The quality of the honey depends on the flowers that are visited by the bees. So beekeepers take heed of the flowering seasons and position their hives accordingly. Here locally, *au verger de la France*, once the plum, cherry, peach, apple, pear, and quince orchards have blossomed, the bees move on to the melon fields. The moment the acacia trees flower, they head for the woods. After that there will be flowering

chestnut, and so the wheel turns. In the hot and arid climate of the French Mediterranean, the bees through the high summer confect potent dark-colored wild-herb honeys of rosemary and thyme. Narbonne has been renowned for its herb-flower honeys since antiquity.

At the Bailey, heather grew on the moors and flowered in July and August. This is the honey that is ingrained as my sensorial reference. It is fragrant, light, and crystalizes into a creamy spreading honey.

The choice of a particular honey conveys a mood and an atmosphere. For a children's table, the subtle flavor of acacia honey might seem appropriate to replace the desire for sugar on strawberries and mint. Dark chestnut or bramble-flower honey is perhaps a better fit for a table of great big burly hunters to eat with their cheese. Whichever honey you choose, be sure to look to the label for floral origin and geographic provenance.

INGREDIENTS
—Serves 6

17 oz. (500ml) milk
6 egg yolks
2 tbsp. (20g) sugar
⅓ cup (110g) honey
6 oz. (175ml) double cream

Proceed as follows, referring to the introductory notes on ice cream (page 230) where and as needed for more detailed instruction.

Bring the milk and some of the sugar up to a simmer. Whisk the egg yolks and remaining sugar together with this simmered sweet milk. Return the resulting proto-custard to the heat, and cook it *à la nappe*. Take it off the heat, and add the honey to infuse; chill the mixture in an iced bain-marie. Pass the mixture through a fine sieve. Add cream and churn.

Vanilla Ice Cream

Vanilla is the fruit of a tropical climbing orchid native to Central America. Like cacao, it was unknown in Europe until brought across the Atlantic by the *conquistadores*.

The fruit that is harvested as vanilla is a long thin pod containing miniscule and highly fragrant seeds. In the wild, these pods fall from the slender flowers of the mother plant to the ground before they are fully ripe. As they dry under the sun, residual liquid is purged through their skin and a process of fermentation occurs within, darkening their color and causing the pods to develop their characteristic fragrance.

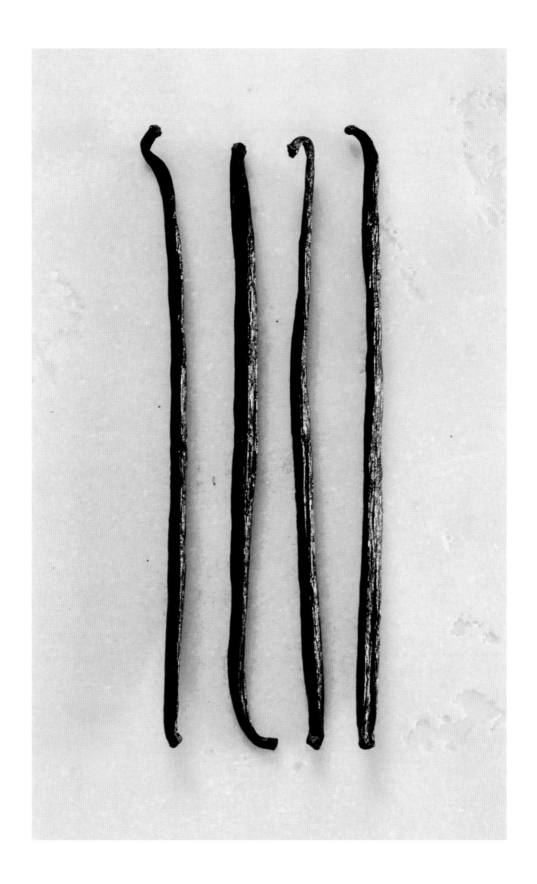

Vanilla planifolia proved mightily tricky to cultivate away from its native Central American forest, as cross-pollination and fertilization depended upon a specific species of indigenous bee. As a result, vanilla remained impossibly rare and expensive until the nineteenth century when an enterprising botanist in Paris developed a technique for artificial pollination. The technique was exported to French colonies of suitable climate, such as Madagascar and Tahiti, where production flourished. Today Madagascar is the world's primary producer.

Labor intensive in the extreme, natural vanilla is the second most expensive spice after saffron. Luckily, a little goes a long way. Vanilla has extraordinary depth of flavor, a complexity of savory, sweet, rich, floral, and astringent earthiness that ambushes the palate. If overdosed it becomes quickly overwhelming.

Most so-called vanilla used in food production is nothing of the sort, but rather synthetic artificial flavoring. This is used on an industrial scale to flavor commercial ice cream. Natural vanilla ice cream, on the other hand, is a delicacy. To do it justice in this recipe be as judicious in the sourcing of quality milk and cream as you are in the purchasing of vanilla pods.

For a lighter finished result I reduce the total quantity of cream used, replacing it in part with yogurt.

INGREDIENTS
—*Serves 6*

14 oz. (400ml) milk
5 oz. (150ml) cream
⅔ cup (130g) sugar
6 egg yolks
3 vanilla pods
½ cup (100g) yogurt

Proceed as follows, referring to the introductory notes on ice cream (page 230) where and as needed for more detailed instruction.

For this ice cream I heat both milk and cream together to optimize the vanilla pod infusion. Open the vanilla pods along the vertical and with the back of a paring knife lift up the seeds that lie within. Add both pods and seeds to the milk, cream, and some of the sugar, and over a moderate flame bring these to a simmer. Then whisk the egg yolks and remaining sugar together with this simmered sweet milk. Return the resulting proto-custard to the heat, and cook it *à la nappe*. Take it off the heat, and stand to infuse, chill the mixture in an iced bain-marie, and add the yogurt. Pass the mixture through a fine sieve and churn.

Strawberry Frozen Yogurt

Frozen yogurt makes for lighter eating than ice cream and is particularly effective with fruit such as strawberries. Here, the flavor of the fruit is demonstrative in a way that it struggles to achieve when competing with milk and cream.

As always, the frozen yogurt you serve is only going to be as good as the base ingredients you use. So in late spring to early summer when the first strawberries ripen, use these. As we progress into June, there will be apricots and then peaches, then use those.

The strawberries we know today were relative latecomers to the kitchen garden. The many varieties of today's garden strawberry all come to us from hybrids of wild strawberries, with larger species brought over from the Americas. Wild woodland strawberries (which have by far the best flavor of any other) were all there were until the eighteenth century, when kings and fancy gardeners transplanted and propagated them for cultivation in an ever more efficient manner.

With the crossing of the Atlantic, native species were brought back to France first from North America and then, in the early eighteenth century, from Chile. Woodland strawberries were hybridized with these larger specimens, thus enabling the emergence of the many varieties of the European strawberry. Today many of the more interesting varieties are only to be found in private gardens. Industrial polythene-tunnel field production prioritizes high yield and early ripening. Reassuringly, wild strawberries persist in the woods, and will happily colonize an area of the garden if left to their own devices.

The yogurt you choose should also be of the best quality you can find. The finest organic yogurt cultured from the milk of the one same herd of mountain sheep, for instance, will only cost a dollar more per pint than some industrial equivalent.

INGREDIENTS
—*Serves 6*

Strawberries to yield 7 oz. (200ml) strawberry pulp
3 ½ oz. (100ml) water
¼ cup (50g) invert sugar (see page 228)
½ cup (95g) sugar
½ tsp. (3g) pectin powder
1 ¾ cups (450ml) yogurt
The juice of a lime

First wash and dry the strawberries. Pass them through a vegetable mill to obtain a pulp. Bring the water together with the invert sugar to the boil, and then add the sugar and the pectin powder. Whisk these together into one homogeneous mass. Stand the resultant syrup to chill upon a nest of ice. Add the strawberry pulp and the yogurt, season with lime juice, and churn. Serve in frozen tumblers, garnished with minted strawberries for the kids. And perhaps nestled into a granita of wild strawberry liqueur—under a sheet of gold leaf—for the grownups.

AND A FEW MORE

SPICED APPLE COMPOTE, YOGURT, ACACIA HONEY

*

CHILLED STRAWBERRY BROTH

*

RHUBARB STEWED WITH GINGER

*

SEARED BANANA, OLIVE OIL & SALT

*

MADEIRA BIRTHDAY CAKE

*

GINGER CRÈME BRÛLÉE

*

FRUIT SALAD

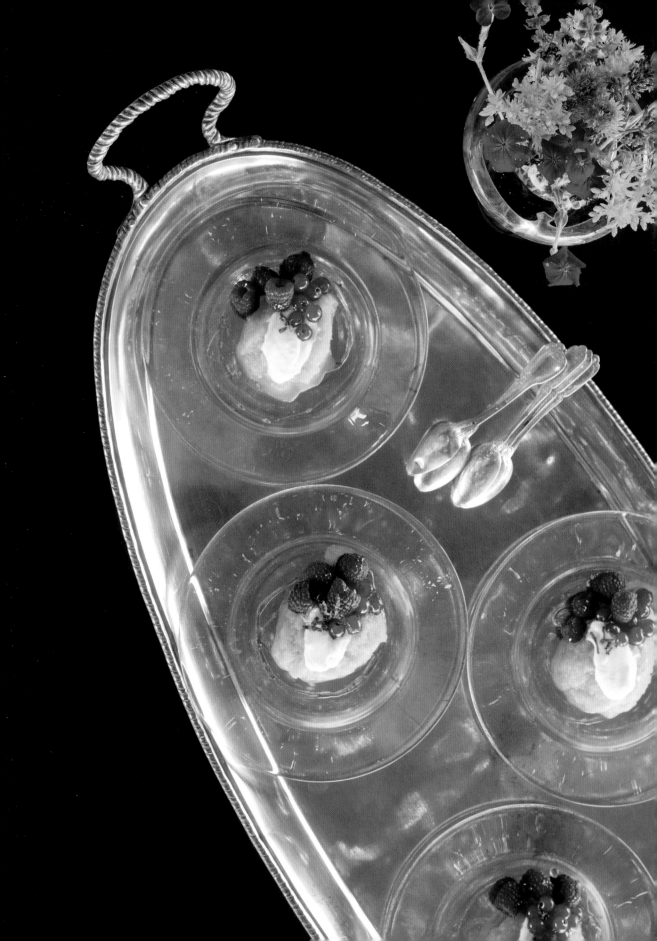

Spiced Apple Compote, Yogurt, Acacia Honey

I often serve fruit compotes spiced with aromatic herbs as dessert. Apple compote spiced with ginger, bay, and chili is one of these. Served with sheep yogurt, garnished with acacia honey, and whatever berries are in season. This makes for a palate-cleansing, almost savory dessert. Not a single crystal of sugar is employed.

INGREDIENTS
—Serves 4

Apples
Mineral water, or apple juice
Bay leaves
Half a mild chili, deseeded
A knuckle of ginger
Berries
Sheep yogurt, or crème fraîche
Mint
Acacia honey, or whichever honey essence you favor

Peel, core, and quarter the apples. Use whichever apples are your favorite; throughout the year this will change, as earlier varieties give way to the better keepers. Chop the apples very fine. You might do this on a mandoline in the same manner we employed for soup. The thinner the apple, the less cooking it will require and so volatile flavors will be optimized.

Place the apples into a saucepan that has a firm-fitting lid. Add half a ladle of mineral water or apple juice to get things started. Add a branch of bay leaves, half of a deseeded chili, a knob or two of ginger, and raise the heat. Once the apple and the aromatics hit the boil, cover the pan with the lid and turn the flame down as low as it will go. With the lid shut, no steam can escape and the aromatics will inform the circulating steam and qualify the compote.

Keep an eye on progress, as you do not want to make an applesauce so spicy no one will eat it. Rather one with a subtle edge of chili that will stimulate and open the palate, for after-dinner nuts and fruit and season's plenty.

Once you are happy with the flavor, remove the lid and reduce the compote to the desired consistency. Pass it through a vegetable mill and that's it. Reserve until needed.

Serve it cold on dessert plates garnished with berries, yogurt or crème fraîche, mint leaves, and honey.

Leftovers will keep well covered in the refrigerator for a couple of days; this makes for a heaven-sent breakfast so be generous with your proportions.

Chilled Strawberry Broth

When strawberries come all together in a glut, and you have already made jam and are no longer quite sure what to do with such a surplus, you can garnish white-wine based cocktails with them. You can make sorbets; you can eat them with clotted cream. But there comes a moment when, for the greater good, you should give rein to your inner bartender.

To Monsieur Verne there is only one way to eat strawberries. Fill a soup plate with them, season with a sprinkling of sugar, and pour red wine over it. It is the sweet version of a classic and invigorating French peasant dish known in the vernacular as *garbure*, a soup bowl of stale bread, over which you pour your glass of wine and eat it up. This recipe for chilled strawberry broth is homage to Monsieur Verne. Note that it is only worth doing with strawberries of the finest quality; otherwise, eat something else. The glory of this dish is in its celebration of the bewitching aroma of strawberry.

INGREDIENTS
—*Serves 4*

Strawberries
Mint
Moonshine, such as grappa
Wild strawberries
Acacia flowers, season permitting
Acacia honey

Clean the strawberries thoroughly of soil and then pass them through a vegetable mill, out of which a thick strawberry broth known in French pastry lingo as a *coulis* will emerge. Do not use a blender, as it will diminish both texture and color. If you are doing this ahead of time, you might steep a bunch of crushed mint in the strawberry broth and let it macerate for an hour or two. Afterwards, wring the mint out thoroughly and press any residue back into the broth through a fine sieve.

To lengthen the broth, dilute it with moonshine. Choose something neutral like grappa. Failing that you could use good vodka. You do not want to make it so strong that your guests crash their cars on the way home. Yet you do want them to stand corrected, in the manner of a shot. Judge one part moonshine to five parts broth, which represents cocktail strength in the region of 17% ABV.

Chill soup plates and garnish them with spiked strawberry broth. Garnish with wild strawberries, and in springtime when the first glut coincides with the flowering of acacia trees, garnish with pert sweet buds of acacia flower, under a golden web of acacia honey.

253

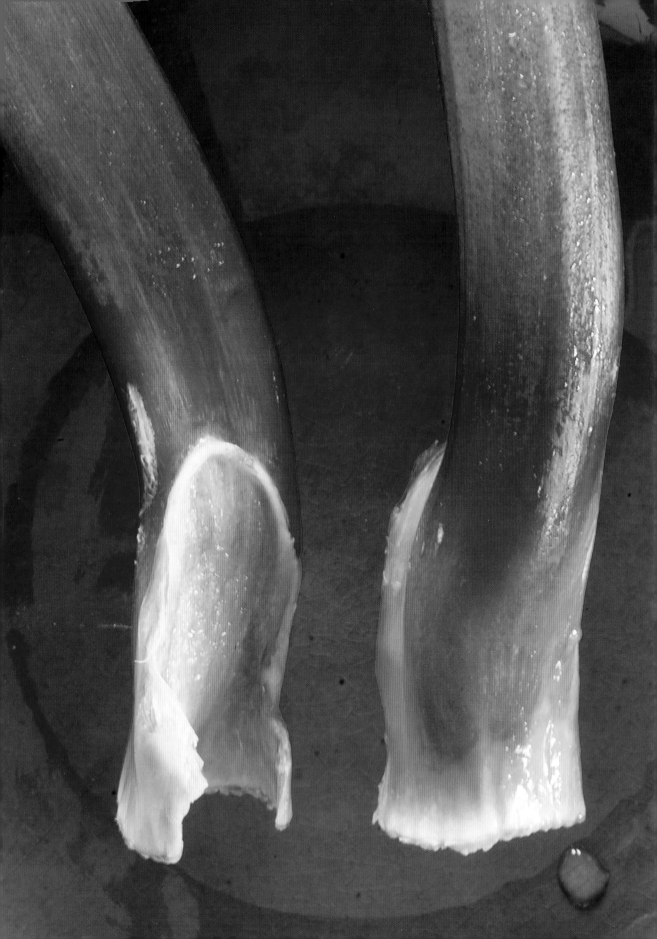

Rhubarb Stewed with Ginger

Rhubarb and ginger are a fine pairing and a very simple dessert to prepare. The rhubarb patch was well kept at the Bailey and this is a dish we ate often as children.

INGREDIENTS
—Serves 4

Rhubarb stalks, leaves removed
Fresh ginger
A pinch of light brown sugar
Mineral water
Crème fraîche, to garnish

Clean the rhubarb under a fast-running tap and stand it to drain. Cut it into inch-long lengths. Put it into a pan over a low flame with slices of fresh ginger. Add a pinch of brown sugar and a ladle of mineral water, just enough to cover the ginger to its waist.

Slowly simmer the rhubarb for quarter of an hour until it surrenders. Resist the urge to touch it too much. The objective is for the rhubarb to hold its form so that you may lift the pieces out intact, seemingly solid to the eye, yet meltingly tender to spoon and palate.

Garnish dessert plates with three or five pieces of rhubarb each, spoon over some of the sweet tart ginger syrup from the pan, and garnish with a generous spoonful of crème fraîche.

Seared Banana, Olive Oil & Salt

If you happen to be in a hemisphere with access to ripe bananas, this is an excellent sweet-savory dessert for a children's table.

INGREDIENTS
—*Serves 4*

Bananas
Extra virgin olive oil
Fleur de sel

Peel bananas and slice them in two along the vertical. Sear them in a nonstick pan in a little olive oil. Once they are gently browned on both sides, lift the bananas from the pan and garnish a serving dish.

Bring them forth to table seasoned with extra virgin olive oil and fleur de sel.

Simple and effective baby food for grownups.

Madeira Birthday Cake

Madeira cake takes its name from Madeira wine. Typically a medium-dry, slightly oxidized, fortified wine made on the Portuguese island of Madeira. In the days before the Suez Canal, Madeira (situated in the Atlantic Ocean several hundred miles off the west coast of Northern Africa) was a port of call to ships traveling east, and this wine was transported all over the world. It was fortified with moonshine to stabilize it for the voyage. The tossing and turning over the high seas exposed the barrels of wine to heat and turbulence, which caused oxidation to occur, giving Madeira wine its distinctive flavor. This aging process of the high seas was later emulated and perfected by the winemakers on dry land, giving us the fine twenty-first-century wine I reference in this recipe.

Its namesake cake, intended for dipping in the wine, is very straightforward to make. It is basically a lemon sponge cake, with whole eggs creamed with the sugar as opposed to just the yolks.

INGREDIENTS
—Serves 6

4 eggs
½ cup (115g) butter
¾ cup (170g) sugar, sifted
The grated zest and juice of an unwaxed lemon
⅞ cup (100g) self-rising flour, sifted
⅝ cup (70g) all-purpose flour

FOR THE FILLING:
Strawberries
Whipped cream
Crème fraîche
Javanese pepper
Mint

Bring the eggs and the butter to room temperature. Weigh all of your ingredients and set them out before you. In a bowl, whisk the eggs together until they are one light mass. Either by hand or with a mixer, cream the softened butter and sifted sugar together into one homogeneous mass. Add the lemon zest. In a steady flow, add the eggs until they too become one with the cake batter. Sift in the mixed flours, and finally add the lemon juice.

Transfer the cake mix to a well buttered, greaseproof-paper-lined circular cake tin and bake it at 350°F (170°C) for an hour. To be sure the cake is cooked through, insert a sharp knife to its heart and look to see if the blade withdraws cleanly. Let the cake rest on a rack until it cools, then turn it out. Counter-intuitively, I am not particularly bothered in this instance how well the cake rises. The objective is to slice it into biscuit-like rounds, which will be built up one upon another.

It goes without saying that wild strawberries will be impossible to outdo as a filling, yet of course they can and will be switched for whatever glut of soft fruit you have to hand. With a whisk to hand whip a quantity of cream into firm peaks. Season this with crème fraîche, grated Javanese pepper, and mint. Then layer: Madeira cake, soft fruit, and cream—floor upon floor—up into leaning tower of birthday cake topped with a candlelit roof.

Ginger Crème Brûlée

Crème brûlée is irresistible. *Nez de cochon*, in French kids' language. Classic juvenile Brasserie behavior is to pick out two holes with a spoon so as it resembles a pig's snout. It is all too often served way too sweet and set too hard, with a thick, palate-smothering layer of caramelized sugar upon it.

At the heart of crème brûlée is custard, usually served in individual ramekins. The key to success is twofold. First, flavor the custard while considering the aftertaste it will leave on the palate. Then cook it very gently in a bain-marie no longer than it takes for the custard to just set. You want the custard to wobble like a natural bosom, not rebound taut like one that's had "work" done.

Crème brûlée is rich in the extreme—sugar and eggs, milk and cream. A tactic to cut through all this is to flavor the custard with an aromatic such as ginger, which will create a clean aftertaste. Essentially it is the same base preparation as ice cream, only you will transform it with heat rather than cold.

INGREDIENTS
—*Serves 10*

12 egg yolks
1 cup (175g) sugar
17 oz. (500ml) milk
3 ½ oz. (100g) knob of ginger, sliced
3 ½ oz. (100g) grated ginger
17 oz. (500ml) double or heavy cream, chilled

CARAMEL CRUST:
Light brown sugar
Castor sugar

First put the egg yolks with one-third of the sugar in a generous-sized bowl. Bring the remaining two-thirds of sugar up to a simmer in the milk along with the sliced ginger, whisking to combine, so that the sugar melts and the sweetened milk becomes one homogeneous mass. Do not let it boil or the flavor will be irreversibly spoiled.

Once this is done, remove the ginger and make your crème anglaise, or custard base. Beat the egg yolks and sugar together stridently. Gently pour the sweetened ginger-flavored milk upon the sugar-blanched egg yolks, all whilst whisking to combine. Start slowly, and then as the mixture amalgamates and becomes one, pour in the rest of the milk in a steady flow, whisking as you go.

Transfer this custard base to a clean saucepan and put it upon a moderate flame. Whisk constantly in a gentle circular motion, bringing the edges of the pan to the center. Have a spatula to hand. The objective is to cook the mixture *à la nappe*. This is determined by dipping the tongue of the spatula into the custard, holding it horizontally, and then running your finger across the sauce coating it. The moment the line retains its straight edge (that is, the sauce does not immediately run over it), it is done. Immediately take the pan off the heat. A moment too long will result in scrambled eggs. Transfer the custard into a clean bowl and add the cold cream and the grated ginger. Stand the mixture to

infuse. Again if left overnight in the refrigerator this will give depth to the infusion and optimize flavor. Garnish ramekins to an elegant height, and place them into a roasting dish. Fill the dish with water (up to the ramekins' waistline) and place it in the oven for one hour at 350°F (180°C).

Once the custard has set, remove the bain-marie from the oven and stand the ramekins to cool. They will hold a day or two quite easily in the refrigerator. The final trick is in building the layers of caramelized crust. This should be done in two stages and with two distinct qualities of sugar: light brown sugar and white castor sugar. You will need a blowtorch to caramelize the tops. First dust the top of the custard with brown sugar, and then turn it upside down so that any excess sugar falls away. Pass the blowtorch over this thin covering of sugar methodically, holding the flame at a distance that allows an even distribution of heat. Once the sugar has caramelized into an even crust, repeat the process with the white castor sugar. The brown sugar gives better texture, while the white sugar better color. The objective is an ephemeral crisp crust of faintly bitter caramel.

Fruit Salad

The key to elegant, textured fruit salad starts with using fruit that is in season, which may seem self-evident but is on the whole quite disregarded. The next consideration is the texture of the fruit itself. Do you want to eat a nectarine with its skin, or would you prefer it peeled? Citrus such as an orange or a lime is vastly more appetizing if you have taken the precaution to lift the fillets from the fibrous body that hold them together as one. In short, the fast track to upgrading a fruit salad lies in dealing with fruits one by one and optimizing their individual textures. A golden sun-kissed apricot skin is rather pleasant and adds certain taste that otherwise might be regretted. Any residue on a grapefruit, on the other hand, is decidedly vile. When you lift the flesh from a melon, it is a false economy in the extreme to think you are penny pinching by riding too close to the rind.

A fruit salad at a five-star-hotel breakfast buffet will look like a repackaged greatest-hits album, archetypes from divergent seasons and climates all corralled as one into an audaciously presented fan. To make matters worse, the generic reflex for dressing a fruit salad is to drown it in sugar syrup in order to camouflage the inherent acidity of out-of-season fruit. Better by far to select the sweetest fruit from amongst your composition, and sacrifice the least eye-catching specimens for juice. Let this be your syrup. Peach juice, the liquid wrung from around a mango pip, in winter a dash of apple juice corrected with a spike of applejack. Focus on the season, and use your imagination. Apply the knife that extends your mind's eye to your hand with thought and design. Measure twice cut once.

It would have been impossible to write this book without the help, support, and encouragement of Susanna Lea, Rizzoli, Charles Miers, Catherine Bonifassi, Christopher Steighner, Julia Wagner, Duncan Campbell, Charlotte Rey, Susan Batson, Alberico Penati, India Jane Birley, Benoit Peverelli, and Molly Malone. Thank you one and all.

First published in the United States of America in 2015
by Rizzoli International Publications, Inc.
300 Park Avenue South
New York, NY 10010
www.rizzoliusa.com

Text and photographs © 2015 Daniel de La Falaise

Design by Campbell-Rey

Illustration on page 3 by India Jane Birley

2015 2016 2017 2018 / 10 9 8 7 6 5 4 3 2 1

Distributed in the U.S. trade by Random House, New York

Printed in China

ISBN-13: 978-0-8478-4484-5

Library of Congress Control Number: 2014956301